This book is dedicated to our families, friends and colleagues who have made our lives truly special events.

Contents

Introduction
What Are We Talking About?

"Usually," "Ordinarily," "Frequently," "Virtually," "Sometimes," "Possibly," "Perhaps."

One of these qualifiers applies to every statement, recommendation, approach, concept, or pronouncement in the following pages. It may not be set in type, but it's there anyway; read every line with these caveats in mind.

Remember: there are almost no absolutes in event marketing.

What produces a notable success in one case can paralyze another. A sizzling success in Tucson might turn out to be a frigid flop in Minneapolis. Furthermore, what works fine for one kind of event in either city can work foul for a different kind of happening in the same city. Even time changes things; the right approach this year is possibly next year's wrong one.

Not even a universally-accepted definition for the term "event marketing" exists. There are as many definitions as there are event marketers. And many professionals either disagree on or have fuzzy understandings of some rather common words, like "advertising," "publicity," and "promotions." But so we can understand each other as we travel together on the following pages, we'll need to agree on some meanings that come pretty close to broad acceptance.

DEFINITION OF TERMS

Event Marketing/Sponsorship

Financial or in-kind support of a non-business related activity, including sports, the arts, festivals, observances, parades, causes, and similar types of activities, usually for the purpose of reaching one or more specified business goals. A special event involves audiences, spectators, or crowds in a recreational pursuit.

Publicity

Obtaining time or space, free *of charge,* in the news media for the purpose of bringing a person, organization, happening, thing, philosophy, image, cause, or other matter to the attention of the general public or segments thereof. Most often, publicity appears within the editorial format of both print and broadcast media.

Advertising

The *purchasing* of time or space in the communications media for the purpose of conveying one or more prescribed messages, usually designed to sell, convince, or move to action. Messages are ordinarily recognizable by distinctive advertising formats in print media and by commercials on television and radio. Outdoor advertising, such as billboards and readerboards also fall under the broader umbrella of advertising.

Promotions

Various marketing techniques aimed at attracting attention to an entity and creating or intensifying a desire for it to be purchased or accepted, usually through incentives. These may included consumer sales enhancers such as sweepstakes, contests, and other proof-of-purchase benefits; product trial opportunities; added value offers; sales force motivators; and retailer incentives; among others.

Event Marketing—Then and Now

The beginning of the special events industry, as we know it today, happened sometime in the mid-1970s, with the exact date and event depending on whom you ask. While some trace sponsorship lineage as far back as Constantine's support of the Circus Maximus, circa 400 A.D. (seating capacity: 250,000, which must have been a marketing nightmare), we prefer to agree with Lesa Ukman, one of the nation's leading experts on event marketing. Ukman credits the birth of event marketing to Fred Lebow, Director of the New York City Marathon. Lebow offered General Motors title sponsorship of the lead car for the marathon in the mid-1970s. Sponsorship Price: $2,000. Answer: No. (Today Mercedes does so: Price tag: $250,000.)

Ukman notes that Jovan brought music into the field with their one-million dollar sponsorship of the Rolling Stones' tour in 1981. Only three years later, in 1984, Pepsi spent five million dollars to sponsor Michael Jackson. It was also in 1984, with Peter Uebberoth's highly publicized and successful efforts involving corporate sponsorship of the Olympic Games in Los Angeles, that the spotlight really turned onto this new and rapidly growing industry. Since that time, corporate sponsorship of events has gone from infancy to adolescence. Having to shake the image of being the new kid on the block and establish its rightful place alongside more traditional forms of marketing, sponsorship has expanded into almost every corner of our lifestyles. Sports, entertainment, arts, and cause-related events, as well as fairs, festivals, and community celebrations of every imaginable theme, keep popping up every year. Although a line forms for every sponsor dollar, companies entering this sponsorship arena are increasing at an equal, if not greater, rate.

Ukman also dramatizes the growth of event marketing since 1984 by noting that in 1988 there were approximately 4,000 companies spending more than 1.8 billion dollars on sponsorships: a four-fold increase in four years! In 1997 North American corporations are expected to spend $5.9 billion on sponsorship ($15.3 billion worldwide), with an estimated continued growth of 10 percent annually.

Ukman notes that about 65 percent of all sponsor dollars goes to sports, mostly to auto racing, with golf in second place and tennis in third. Entertainment tours and attractions receive 11 percent, while nine percent goes to sponsorship of festivals, fairs and annual events. Approximately six percent goes to the arts and nine percent to cause

marketing. Spending on sponsorships continues to outpace the growth of traditional media by three to four percent.

Event marketing and sponsorship are today where public relations was nearly three decades ago. Each year, more companies and events realize the value of this young industry, which some experts call the fourth marketing medium, and yet still very few of those entering the field are properly equipped to deal effectively in it.

In its $5.9 billion dollar adolescence, the special events industry is still often unsteady on its feet, and some strengthening is needed. There are virtually no formal training programs, although some are currently being developed. Relatively little information is available to the industry, but existing sources are well used. There are some seminars, which offer opportunities to hear speakers and trade war stories, but many are one-sided presentations that use more "show and tell" than "how-to" approaches. Audiences leave feeling more frustrated or overwhelmed rather than more capable of doing their jobs.

Sponsors and sponsees are both still working on their ever-changing formulas, and a few have abandoned the quest, but savvy marketers are using event marketing more and more effectively. That, of course, will attract talented and better trained newcomers. Despite all the growing pains, there is no question that event marketing is here to stay and that its future is a bright one. It is an exciting time to be a part of this developing industry.

Our purpose in writing this book is to formalize or crystallize a wide range of thinking relative to the strategy of event marketing. It is our goal to present a condensed, viable, and totally practical "how-to" approach to securing corporate sponsorships and to making events as successful, easily implemented, and rewarding as they can be.

While we have attempted to write this book to be of value to those who have little or no experience in event marketing, we have also tried to offer new ideas, fresh thinking, and creative approaches that will be worthwhile to those with some experience as well as those who are highly polished professionals.

Our intention is to help you make all of your events very special ones.

Chapter One

WHAT'S IN IT FOR ME?

INDISPENSABLE SUPPORT

Virtually no present-day event of any size can survive without at least some financial support from commercial sponsors, and most require much more than token sponsorship. This support can return numerous benefits to the sponsoring organization, but the bottom-line impact on the event itself can mean the difference between success and failure.

Many companies are happy to provide sponsorship support—monetary, in-kind, or both—when they can be shown graphically and conclusively that their participation will significantly help them meet one or more of their corporate objectives. While some sponsorship decisions are made on an emotional level, rarely will a company provide any sizable amount of support without justifiably expecting—and receiving—a meaningful business return of some kind on its investment.

The answer to "What's in it for me?" from an event-production viewpoint is clear. Financial support from a commercial sponsor helps to cover expenses, keep patron costs down, and insure quality and longevity of the event. "What's in it for me?" from a sponsor's viewpoint is quite different. For a sponsor, an event can do the following:

- Create positive publicity
- Heighten visibility
- Set sponsor apart from its competition
- Complement other marketing programs
- Enhance image
- Shape customer attitudes
- Improve customer relations
- Sell or sample products/services directly
- Drive traffic
- Increase employee morale/quality of life
- Fulfill responsibility as good corporate citize.
- Contribute to community economic development
- Combat larger advertising budgets of competitors
- Reach specifically targeted markets

SETTING SPONSORSHIP OBJECTIVES

When a company considers sponsorship, especially for the first time, it is important first to set objectives that you hope will be realized as a result. Events seeking sponsorship should help potential sponsors define objectives if they have not done so themselves. Without clear objectives, there can be no logical method for a sponsor to consider sponsorship or measure the success of sponsorship after the event. In most cases, the result will be that the sponsor or the event (usually the sponsor) gets burned because no one took time to decide what tangible results were desired. Clear objectives equal success in a number of ways, as shown in the box on the next page.

THE VALUE OF CLEAR OBJECTIVES

Clear Objectives	=	Easier Sponsorship Selection
Clear Objectives	=	Easier Development of Original Concepts
Clear Objectives	=	Easier Sell to Top Management
Clear Objectives	=	Easier Total Implementation
Clear Objectives	=	Easier Measurement of Results
Clear Objectives	=	Easier Ties with Advertising, Public Relations
Clear Objectives	=	Easier Gauge of Future Sponsorship

Generally, companies incorporate one or more of seven broad objectives when they judge sponsorship opportunities. We surveyed a cross section of corporate sponsors, representing a wide range of business interests, and asked them to list their top objectives for sponsorship. Their responses indicated the following objectives and order of preference.

1.   To Enhance Image/ Shape Consumer Attitudes

It is often important for a company to improve or maintain the way it is seen by customers, stockholders, and the general public. By associating itself with high-quality events, particularly those appealing to broad interests and offering appropriate public credit to sponsors, a company achieves this goal.

2.   To Drive Sales

For many types of sponsors, events offer a potent force for selling or sampling large quantities of products or services in a short period of time with minimum distribution requirements. In addition to allowing sponsors to showcase product attributes, this selling /sampling also promotes future sales. Sponsors with sales as an objective should expect to pay a sponsorship fee plus a percentage of the sales. Sampling rights are often offered as part of a larger benefits package. Being called the "official" beverage, food, service, etc. of an event can be expensive, but worth the money in many cases.

On-site sales/sampling can also be supplemented with other pre- and post event sales promotions to drive in-store traffic. Redeemable coupons can be distributed, especially for services, packaged goods, or frozen foods that are not easily accommodated in an event setting; and retailer/trade incentives can also be created around the event.

Proof of purchase is another promotion option. Boxtops or labels can be redeemed at an event or other location for admission, souvenir merchandise, or food tickets. These can be purchased in advance by the sponsor or reimbursed to the promoter following the event.

In all of the above, it should be the responsibility of the sponsor to promote this kind of event participation. On-site bannering, program listings, and publicity provided by the event should serve to amplify sponsor efforts."

3.   To Obtain Positive Publicity/ Heighten Visibility

Virtually all consumer-driven operations include this objective in their goals line-up. It is important for them to have their product, service or company identified favorably in a public manner as frequently as possible. In the jargon of the marketing world, they want "warm fuzzies" to surround whatever they are selling.

Event marketing has been found to be one of the most effective means of generating positive publicity. An event often creates news about "a something" when there would otherwise be no news about it.

Caution: News media resist exaggerated efforts to get brand names mentioned in their columns or during air time. Therefore, reasonable approaches and expectations must be in the minds of both events and sponsors. Media in most host cities are fair in their coverage of event activities, especially those that are in the nonprofit category. Many are sponsors themselves. Thus, some barriers to commercialism can be removed

4. To Differentiate Product from Competitors

It is important to sponsors that consumers differentiate their product or service from their competitors', especially at the time of purchase. Events allow them to create an affiliation with a specific target audience(s) at the "lifestyle level" that will hopefully translate to purchasing decisions later.

Among the market segments most often targeted by companies are:

- •Rural populations
- •Senior citizens
- •Young people
- •Ethnic minorities
- •Employees/Retirees
- •Women
- •Families

5. To Help with Good Corporate Citizen Role

More and more, companies are taking seriously their responsibilities to the communities in which they reside or serve. They feel they owe residents more than payrolls and taxes. Sponsoring events is an especially viable instrument for achieving this goal in that events are usually available to a wide range of people, throughout the community.

The other side of this very valuable coin is to enhance the quality of life for their employees. High-quality events add to the free-time options and volunteer opportunities for employees and their families, and sponsorship by a specific business can add to higher employee pride, participation and morale.

Even if publicity is not a primary goal, good corporate citizens must be publicly credited at every opportunity—through media, program mention(s), etc. Events should give as much credit as is appropriate.

6. To Contribute to Community Economic Development

If the community in which a company operates prospers, so does that company. This is especially true for such service industries as telephone companies, utilities, banks, and real estate agencies. The same goes for many consumer-driven endeavors such as supermarkets, pharmacies, malls, hotels, restaurants, and retail stores.

A direct influence on economic development is the quality of life in a community. Employers like to be in an environment where their people feel happy, safe, and content, and where they have appealing free-time opportunities. A well-designed, well-run event contributes significantly to that quality of life.

An event also plays a measurable monetary role as well, one that directly contributes to the host city's economic health through the influx of tourists and tourism dollars, in addition to local dollars that may not be spent if the event did not exist. Tourists use virtually no tax-supported functions— schools, city facilities, public services, etc.—but they do leave money behind that supports those needs for local residents. Most importantly, merchants and other local commercial enterprises benefit directly from tourist expenditures.

7. To Enhance Business, Consumer and VIP Relations

Many businesses buy into events in order to obtain preferential treatment for important present and potential customers. Perks such as choice reserved seating, special receptions, back stage passes, golf rounds, and other hospitality benefits ingratiate customers to sponsoring businesses and suppliers. A related goal is to influence government leaders, thought-promoters, and other VIPs important to the sponsoring company. The ability to satisfy these special needs should be a primary sales point during efforts to garner event sponsorships.

Those soliciting sponsorship for events should realize that every candidate sponsor could have all seven objectives. Possible objectives of various sponsors are outlined in the box on the following page. When targeting a potential sponsor, it is important to highlight benefits that correspond to the company's probable major objectives.

Obviously, there can be exceptions within each category, but the grouping in the opposite column is meant to serve as a general guideline. Narrowing can be done when more research has been completed on prospective sponsors.

CANDIDATE TYPE	PROBABLE MAJOR OBJECTIVES
Supermarkets	1,2,4,6,7
Food product/Snacks	1,2,4,7
Hotels	2,3,4,6
Soft Drinks	1,2,4,7
Beer	1,2,3,4,7
Fast Food	2,4,6
Credit Card	1,2,3,4,7
Banks/Financial Institutions	1,2,3,4,5,6,7
Hospitals	1,3,4,5
Oil Companies	2,4,5
Camera/Film	1,2,4,7
News Media	1,2,3,4,5,6,7
Retailers	1,2,4,6
Auto Dealerships	1,2,4,5,6
Airlines	1,2,4,7
Telephone/Cellular	1,2,3,4,5,6,7

■ SECTION 1 ■

CREATING YOUR OWN EVENT

CHAPTER TWO

TO BE OR NOT TO BE?

SHOULD WE EVEN DO AN EVENT?

Hard investigative work is required before this question can be answered. Wanting to do an event is not reason enough to do it; that desire should merely be the motivation to find out whether an event should be tried.

In most cases, event feasibility studies should be conducted by qualified professionals. They know what to look for, are adept at ferreting out sources and information quickly and easily, can provide meaningful projections based on current knowledge, and are able to weave many findings into one end result.

More importantly, these "outsiders" are more objective than those involved in event planning and production who might try their hand at conducting a feasibility study. The professional's reputation rests on giving the appropriate answer—yes or no—to the question of whether an event should be scheduled.

FEASIBILITY STUDY LEAD TIME

One of the biggest, most frequent problems in the event industry is timing. Event producers often try to stage their happenings before they're ready. Many wait too long to try to sell sponsorships, which is discussed extensively elsewhere in this book.

Those needing to conduct a feasibility study are also often caught in a time-vise. A study takes from a minimum of a few weeks to several months or even a year, particularly if a master plan is called for at the completion of the study.

Then comes implementation. Major efforts are required for organizing an administrative group; lining up and training volunteers; locating talent, equipment, supplies, and facilities; printing brochures; and so forth. Weeks and months will be consumed even for a relatively small happening.

In short, most events of any dimension should not be fielded until a year or more after completion of the feasibility studies that determine the ideal dates of presentation. This is especially true for large, new events.

ESSENTIAL QUESTIONS FOR A FEASIBILITY STUDY

The following questions are considered to help those working with professional feasibility study consultants, or to guide those who feel capable of conducting their own. Answers must be objective and based on solid, current, factual information.

What types of events should be considered?

Perhaps you already have an event type in mind. If so, the study already has a target. But nothing should be so pre-sold that objectivity is neutralized. If thinking is along general lines, all options should be studied to determine which type of event—city wide, neighborhood, arts, food, sports, etc.—will have the greatest appeal and the greatest likelihood of success.

What determinants should be studied?

Whether a specific type of event is being studied or the search is on for the best type to attempt, there are several factors that must be carefully researched, analyzed, and weighed.

Weather

Even if the activity is staged indoors, weather should strongly influence event timing. For example, many people do not like to drive in snow or get soaked walking to an enclosed arena. Obviously, weather is a greater consideration for outdoor events. Research should help select a time when the candidate area has better than an 80 percent chance of having the kind of weather that would promote attendance and facilitate event presentation.

Best sources for weather information are the nearest office of the United States Weather Service, Chamber of Commerce records and promotional material, university and airport meteorological stations, newspaper morgues and public libraries. Weather records going back 25 years or more should be studied.

Competition

Other events that exist or are planned that could siphon off attendance and attention must be carefully studied. Consideration should not be limited to those activities that are directly competitive; any offering that could interfere with one in the candidate location should be examined. If a popular sporting event is set for the dates being considered, other dates should be explored.

Since most events rely heavily on publicity to attract crowds, new events should be timed to be as far removed as possible from media space and-time eaters that are already established. Otherwise, a fledgling event would have a particularly tough time getting attention.

Major national happenings can also have an effect on local attendance end publicity. Anyone setting an unrelated event on Super Bowl Sunday afternoon would probably be unsuccessful. National political conventions are big consumers of local media attention as well, taking time and space that would be available for other coverage, such as the proposed event.

The importance of proximity of competition correlates closely with population. Simultaneous events in the California cities of Santa Monica and Santa Ana do not rival one another because not only are they 50 miles apart, but they are also within a heavily-populated metropolitan area.

However, two same-time events scheduled in Wichita, Kansas, for example, would compete with each other for attendance.

Primary sources for competitor information include Chamber of Commerce event calendars, tourism-promotion material, newspaper morgues, the International Festivals & Events Association, Chase's Annual Events, and The IEG Sponsorship Source Book (See Special Section B).

Population

Whether the event is a Vivaldi chamber orchestra concert or one of the dimensions of the Pasadena Tournament of Roses Parade, there must be enough interested people available to support it. This is especially true when admission is charged.

Demographic research is of paramount importance in a feasibility study. First, the total number of people living within the event marketing radius must be determined. For a citywide festival, that radius is generally 100 miles, a comfortable two-hour drive. For many state fairs, however, the entire state comprises the marketing area, because many attendees enjoy multiple-day fair visits.

Just counting people, though, isn't enough. Factors especially important to the proposed event, such as average income, age strata, unemployment percentages, ethnic and minority groupings, and predictions for growth or decline of those and all pertinent categories over the next decade, need to be considered as well. The demographic pattern of the studied locale should fit virtually all needs of the event under consideration. If it does not, another event type or perhaps even a no-event decision is warranted.

Such information may be obtained from the United States Census Bureau, statistical abstracts prepared by state and local governmental offices, Chambers of Commerce, and *The Rand McNally Commercial Atlas & Marketing Guide*.

If the proposed event is in a sports category, check with its national association; almost every sport of any size has one. The national organization can often provide local contacts or offer information to help determine whether the area has enough supporters for the event. The same is true of many cultural organizations.

Of course, there should already be a reason an event is being considered. Enough Vivaldi devotees are likely to have made themselves known to spawn someone's interest in staging a Vivaldi concert. If not, and if the event is hinged entirely on speculation, organizers will probably have to "paper the house" (give away tickets to help fill seats).

Attitudes

How do those targeted to attend or participate in the event feel about it? Do many golfers think there are already too many tournaments in the area? Do law enforcement officials feel a major citywide festival will overtax an already overtaxed police force?

Though more subjective than other determinants, attitude is no less an important one. And the only truly effective way any degree of attitude measurement can be formulated is through personal interviews.

Questionnaires asking recipients how they feel about a proposed event are nearly always futile. In most cases, recipients fail to respond. Of those who do, many have given little thought to their answers or have been confused (which often results in negative attitudes) because a questionnaire rarely affords an opportunity to spell out an adequate event description. For that last reason, news media polls should never be used to gauge public reaction to an event idea.

Well-designed personal interview strategies produce meaningful attitude profiles. Interviews require deft handling and often take a considerable amount of time. These factors suggest the efficacy of hiring professionals to conduct such studies, especially if a major event is contemplated. Those selected for interviews may include leaders or representatives of commerce and industry, cultural and financial pursuits, civic and fraternal clubs, religious and educational groups, and law enforcement and government agencies. Certainly members of the specialized organizations directly related to the theme of the proposed event, such as golf associa-

tions, softball leagues, or opera guilds should be included. Following are some interview tips.

- Generally, interviews should not be recorded. Regardless of their degree of sophistication, many interviewees "play to the microphone." Often, people aren't as spontaneous and candid when they are being taped.
- If appropriate, at the outset of each meeting, interviewees should be assured that their responses will remain confidential or will be approved by them before being made public and that they, as sources, will remain anonymous.
- Interview sessions should last an hour or less. Questions should be written and in hand, but they should not be sent to subjects ahead of the interview unless factual information that must be researched is needed.
- Questions should be worded so that they encourage a narrative response rather than a simple yes or no.
- If an interview tends to "take off on its own," it should either be 1) pulled back to the right direction, or 2) allowed to continue as long as the subject matter is being properly, sufficiently, and succinctly covered and the interview feels comfortable to both parties. Multiple-interviewee sessions are less desirable. When more than two respondents are present, frequently the "leader influence syndrome," accompanied by the "me, too" reaction, comes into play. A more forceful interviewee can sway other respondents and thus contaminate results.
- Adequate notes should be taken, but not at the expense of breaking the flow of the exchange. So that the respondent does not have to wait, keyword reminder notes should be used by the interviewer.
- Notes should be transcribed before they grow cold, which they tend to do quickly.
- When possible, transcripts should be sent to interviewees for fact checks, particularly if figures have been given.

Facilities and Services

Determine the answers to the following facilities and services questions to ensure a successful, safe event.

- If the event will concentrate large numbers of people in a compact area, will that area be sufficient, efficient, and safe for attendees? If not, what alternatives are available?
- Can vehicular and pedestrian traffic patterns be controlled effectively?
- Can law enforcement agencies handle the additional demands of the event?
- Do adequate facilities exist that can accommodate event needs, such as auditoriums, stages, arenas, parks, and playing fields? Will they be available?
- Can additional facility needs be met through leases, rentals, or construction?
- Are there sufficient personnel—paid and volunteer—to implement event plans successfully?
- Are there those with expertise and work specialties needed by the event who can be hired or whose talents can be donated?
- What services are available for the removal of refuse and for keeping the event area clean, safe, and attractive?

Community Support

Again, a fairly subjective determinant must tee considered: how supportive is the community of special events? Assuming that reasonable quality happenings are offered, questions that should be answered in the affirmative include these:

- Are there usually good turnouts for events, free and paid?
- Does the community seem to have a good level of genuine enthusiasm for such activities?
- Do local media give reasonable coverage to events?
- Have governmental regulatory agencies been cooperative in helping with events, such as rescinding or passing ordinances that facilitate event functioning?
- Do local organizations, including civic and fraternal clubs, youth groups, and others, get behind events in a meaningful manner?

Community Reputation

Proposed events have a much better chance of flourishing if they are to take place in cities or neighborhoods with earned reputations for reasonable lodging, food, and merchandise price structures; cleanliness; low-crime rates; and friendly people. If the feasibility study deals with a venue where any of these assets are lacking—and if the problem(s) cannot be easily corrected well in advance of the event—serious consideration should be given to holding plans in abeyance.

Sponsorships

It bears repeating: very few events of any dimension today can be fielded without some measure of financial support from the corporate community. Funds provided through company event budgets or foundations play a large and growing role in event revenue support, and every indication points to a continuation of that growth. The feasibility study should virtually pivot on the availability of sponsorships, unless some remarkable formula for subsidizing the proposed event does not include the need for corporate dollar support.

The study should report on the history of such backing by local firms. It should list them and suggest the likelihood of their financial involvement in the planned event. Local "most likely" sponsors should be listed first, but if the activity is big enough to warrant attention from national sponsors, reports of investigations into best candidates at that level should comprise a chapter in a feasibility study. Sources for such information are covered in Special Section B.

IF THE ANSWER IS "NO"

If the feasibility study has been properly conducted and its findings correctly directed into a conclusion, there will be an answer to the question: "Should we have a special event?"

If the answer is negative, the reasons should be shared with those who have a right to know: members of a committee assembled to consider the question, individuals who have been pushing for an event, and perhaps the media, if they have been aware of the study.

The fact that a study was launched means that one or more people thought an event would be a good idea, so disappointment when a negative result is announced can be expected. Those personally involved in conducting the study or supervising the consultant who has done it should know every line of the resulting document and the rationale behind it well enough to defend it and the bottom-line findings. It's common to have to do so.

IF THE ANSWER IS "YES"

If the outcome is that hoped-for "yes" response, work has only begun. There is now a road map to the event; the trip—the really big effort—is yet to be made.

A complete "yes" feasibility study will reveal one or more of the most suitable events for your locale and circumstances, or it will support the kind you had in mind. If it is a comprehensive study, it should do the following:

- recommend the exact dates and times for the event;
- propose a location for the event, unless a pre-study venue was specified;
- give the event a carefully selected name, if requested;
- outline and arrange a schedule of event elements, if that need was specified in the contract;
- formulate a thorough budget;
- spell out start-up need and next steps;
- target audiences;
- provide a reasonably complete marketing plan;
- include a fairly detailed strategy for eliciting sponsorships;
- list sources or suppliers for such needs as tents, portable generators, walkie-talkies, etc.;

- suggest the most logical organizational pattern of management, committees, volunteers, etc.; and
- project where the event should go in the next five or ten years in terms of attendance, budgets, themes, organization, staff, etc.

All these elements must be specified clearly in the consultant contract or in the outline of the study one plans to conduct.

COST OF A STUDY

As is true of almost everything, one gets what one pays for in a feasibility study. The consultant can be instructed to delineate only whether an event will likely be successful and the reasons for that finding. Or, the subjects listed earlier can be fully covered, with a full-blown masterplan if the study suggests that an event is feasible.

In the first instance, for a minimal of "yes" or "no" effort, fees and expenses should range from $2,500 to $5,000. For the full-range study and master plan, totals span from around $15,000 to more than $25,000. Intermediate-caliber studies, depending on scope, cost between $5,000 and $15,000.

KEEP IT HANDY

Too frequently, the "yes" feasibility study presentation is read by those who arranged for it, causing an initial flurry of enthusiasm and high interest. Then, it's laid aside and rarely referred to again. The report should be regularly consulted and its recommendations carefully followed.

CHAPTER THREE

YOUR EVENT OR MINE?

SPONSORING EXISTING EVENTS VERSUS CREATING YOUR OWN

Most sponsoring organizations back existing events. It's easy to understand why, although some of the reasons may be a little less than logical:

- Existing events are established and thus probably less risky. There's usually no need to launch heavy, possibly expensive promotional efforts to make them go.
- Implementation is usually easier. Sponsors often want as little labor involvement as possible because staffs are already working at near-capacity on other assignments.
- Many event-production staffs include worldclass salespersons. They are masters at garnering sponsor dollars even when, at times, their established event is a poor fit for their benefactors.
- The CEO is big on golf and determines that his company will support his pet sport. Of course, he wants a tie-in of which he can be proud, so his people go after the best already-established golf tournament available. (For "golf", you can also read "opera," "sailing," "art shows," "tennis," "race cars," etc.)
- Competitors have latched on to a given prestigious event, which apparently is a successful sponsorship match, so why not do the same?

- Uncle John is on an existing event's board of directors. He pressures his highly placed kin to bring in backing from their employers.
- Sponsors recognize that they're not in the events-production industry and prefer to leave it up to those who are.
- And finally..."Failure stains someone else, not me."

WHY DO YOUR OWN THING?

But what about creating an event? Why shouldn't that be considered? Here are some reasons self-created events can be the best promotional avenues to take.

- Very careful study of the total marketing communications program might indicate that a self-created event will satisfy a need that no other medium can under present conditions. Perhaps budgets are too limited to permit another flight of advertising but will allow for the less expensive production and marketing of an event. Or maybe an event will create "news" where none exists, thus enlarging publicity opportunities; or maybe it will tie well into an existing premium offer.
- Everything points to the feasibility of plugging into an event, but no event tailored to the company's purposes and objectives exists.
- With a self-created event, the sponsor owns it. It can be what the sponsor wants it to be—

what's best for the company and its objectives. By owning an event, the title slot is entirely the sponsor's. Or other names can be added to the credit list with the sponsor's name always at the top and in bigger letters.

- By working from initial concept, a sponsor can—and should—pattern the event precisely to meet its objectives and needs. It can say what the company wants said—exactly. Size, reach, location, timing, cost, and all other elements are completely at the discretion of the sponsor.

- By filling a void in a community's event calendar with the right type of offering, the sponsor can have the local show to itself for its duration. The public, the media attention, the promotional ties, and the dollars from lesser sponsors all belong to the creating sponsor.

- Fear of owned-event development and implementation need not be an issue. There are several event production companies throughout the nation that can conceptualize an event with a company and follow through with full implementation and measurement. Most have reasonable fees. If there isn't one in the local area, call on people who have had successful experiences in the field of interest, such as a college drama faculty; those who have staged appropriate athletic events (professional or collegiate); or booking and staging personnel at local arenas, sports centers, auditoriums, little theatres, stadiums, etc. Professional associations related to the type of event envisioned can be very helpful in locating production people. These include the International Festivals & Events Association, the International Events Group, and national organizations dealing with golf, tennis, and other sports.

DRAWBACKS?

There are some drawbacks, of course.

- As noted in the section on quality, too many people who don't know what they're doing try to stage events. If the activity is a neighborhood pot-luck get-together, a seasoned, professional event producer will hardly be needed. However, if plans get much bigger than that, start thinking about getting some-

one who can really do the job well. Few sponsoring organizations have qualified personnel on their staffs who can conceive and successfully implement plans for an event worthy of carrying the corporate name. Outside help is nearly always required.

- Event general contracting is very time consuming. If a company is looking at doing its own happening, its staffing status should be carefully studied before a decision is made. If not, the result may be an unhappy, overworked crew and a lousy event.

- A new event does not enjoy the advantage of word-of-mouth promotion, always the best event sales tool. A higher percentage of dollars will have to be spent on marketing a new offering than on marketing an established one.

EXAMPLES OF SUCCESSFUL SELF-CREATED EVENTS

On the Road

In the early 1980s, child safety was an especially hot topic. A major packager of children's cereals wanted to contribute to that effort while tastefully publicizing its brands. Advertising was consigned to other topics and could not be redirected. Publicity was stymied because there would be little to say (unless there was some major peg on which to hang more media-attraction material such as an event), and the commercialism barrier would hamper product mention in the media.

Objectives were met with the creation, by the company, of a show designed to play at malls throughout the nation. The 25-minute free production featured marionette versions of the children's cereal characters, brought together in a cute and kid-appealing show that put across a number of child safety messages. Booked into 52 malls in as many weeks, it was an exceptional success.

A check with a major theme park, noted for the excellent quality of its character costumes, revealed the name of the costume designer, who was contacted. Fortunately, the designer's company was capable of making the marionettes, producing the show, and booking the malls, most of which that company had worked with previously. An effective public relations agency, noted for success in special event publicity, was hired. Two members of the corporate public relations office were assigned to oversee the project, thus keeping staff involvement to a minimum.

Because only about 600-800 people would see the show at each presentation, the event was designed to appeal to television talk show producers and to provide grist for the newspaper editorial mills. Representatives of the show served as spokespersons, taking marionettes to talk shows and being interviewed for print media, thus providing brand-specific credit while promoting safety tips. Additionally, the timeliness of the topic and animated nature of the presentation magnetized considerable TV news coverage, with crews shooting the shows at malls to get their footage.

In addition to strong and successful efforts by the public relations agency, arrangements with malls required them to promote appearances through their own advertising and publicity. The final audited results showed that nearly 200 million combined media impressions were garnered by this event and its attendant publicity. It cost the company less than two dollars to reach each one thousand people. And the malls were delighted with the highly professional caliber of this production that significantly increased their traffic and greatly enhanced their publicity programs.

Event Promotes Event

A large, regional business-to-business company regularly helps sponsor a major golf tournament, contributing up to one million dollars yearly. Its primary sponsorship goal is to entertain major business customers, thanking them for past purchases and hoping to lure future ones.

After a few years of participation, the company decided that it should reap publicity benefits as well. But there was a formidable problem: this corporation was one of several tournament sponsors, all big names and all coming up with the same amount of funding. This cluster resulted in some signage credit on site and on a few billboards around the host community, but rarely were the sponsors named in media coverage.

Advertising budgets were limited; no funds were available for anything but selling the company's services. Publicity efforts to have the media note the company's participation failed to get past commercial barriers. The event itself was not getting sufficient name-mention in the media. The answer: self-create an event. As it turned out, three back-up events were suggested in support of the major one.

Arrangements between sponsors and the hosting golf course gave each organization a large number of free-play holes each year. The course also committed to spend several thousand dollars on those playing those holes.

The suggested strategy called for the company to use those arrangements to stage three regional, pre-event invitational tournaments, all sponsored by just the single corporation. One would be for women, the second for senior citizens, and the third for teenagers. To enhance the company image, strategy called for each tournament to be given a cause-marketing hinge. Income from each of the events would be donated to charities serving the groups involved in each tournament, such as aid for single mothers, senior citizen health programs, and teenage job-search efforts.

With considerable help from the golf course staff, the events were to be designed by the public relations staff, with implementation handled entirely by employee volunteers under public relations staff supervision. With the no-cost course arrangement, the course financial contribution available for awards and incidentals, all person-power provided by volunteer employees, and proceeds from ticket sales and admissions going to the charities, the pre-event events cost the company virtually nothing.

Strategy called for these events to be held two weeks ahead of the major PGA tournament as a means of drawing attention to the fact that their sponsor is also a major backer of the larger tournament. That approach would add prestige to the smaller trio. Promotion was to be done through carefully-angled publicity material which, because of the charity tie-ins, would find much easier receptions in editorial offices. Coverage in other than sports pages was highly desirable. Hometown releases on participants—participation announcements, follow-ups on winners—would help spread the word throughout the company's regional marketing area.

Moral: the publicity game can be won through a company's innovative strategy, built on one or more self-created events.

SOME IMPORTANT REMINDERS

Whether the event is established or self-created, the following facts apply.

- Signing a sponsorship or event-producdon check and walking away without writing one for its support and promotion is half-strategy. Be prepared to put from 50 percent (for a local, mid-level event) to as much as 500 percent (for a major, international event) of the sponsorship price-tag toward its promotion.

- Don't forget to define objectives. That is the only way to know which way to go and whether the destination has been reached.
- Don't be sponsor-fickle. Tying into an event once or twice, then deciding it's not for your company and moving to another is a waste of money. In most instances, the rule is to stick with an event for at least three or four trials, unless failure is a certainty or there are other very serious mitigating circumstances.
- Conduct or buy a feasibility study before creating an event, and research existing events before sponsoring them.

Chapter Four

A MATTER OF QUALITY

THE DEFINITIVE NEED

Too many events today are bad. Or, at least, they're not as good as they should and could be. Many of their promoters and administrators have fooled themselves and some others into believing that their happenings are big successes, pointing to large audience turnouts, generous media coverage, corporate sponsorship support and nice words from spectators or audience members. On the surface, their claims of success appear to be valid.

But in reality, that "success" is by default. Perhaps there simply isn't anything else for people to do during the run of the event. They're not necessarily being offered something of value. The event is merely something different to do, a break in the routine, a chance to "get out for awhile." Frequently, there's no basis for comparison between same-type events, so participants just don't know that an event is mediocre or only slightly better.

Most tourists will not return to a ho-hum event. Tourists, however, are very often the primary marketing targets of event producers. Tourism's "new dollars" are highly desirable to any community, so promotional efforts and money must be directed to bringing in visitors.

Try asking producers to reveal substantiated economic-impact studies of their events, spotlighting how many local people and tourists attended and how much money they spent during its run. One will frequently be given any of the following answers:

- "We've never had one done; they're too expensive."
- "We really don't need one, we already know we have a winner."
- "Such information is confidential."
- "The one we had done was inconclusive."

Many event administrators either are afraid to commission an economic impact study, fearing the revelation of poor financial truth, or have bought such studies and want to bury the distressing results. The reason dollar-flow information is often so scary is because it can prove events to be less economically effective than their administrators may claim.

Media frequently determine news value by attendance and, if nothing else is going on, will cover an event that draws a crowd. Often that coverage is a response to civic duty, tradition, or habit. Introduce new, high-quality competition, however, and see which event gets the greater amount of media time and space.

Sponsors, perhaps feeling the pull of civic responsibility and being aware of thousands of participants, are willing to buy into the event. For awhile, anyway. But again, offer them a more creative or polished event and they will take their dollars to it because that's where the people and the media go.

WHAT CAUSES POOR EVENTS?

One large U.S. festival claims to attract 250,000 participants annually. (There are those who challenge that number, saying its inflation ratio may be as much as 30 percent). Its promoters regularly claim success, pointing to its popularity among people, the media, and sponsors.

Yet when a consultant screening American events for a feasibility study requested information on the economic impact of that event on its community, a festival insider quietly admitted that the last impact survey, done three years before, produced such embarrassing results that its findings were squelched and a decision was made to avoid such studies, at least in the near future.

Like so many of its counterparts, their event is tired. It hasn't had an infusion of creative energy in years. Its elements are the same year after year. From one summer to the next, the parades, entertainment, sporting events, marathon run, kite contests, etc., are virtually identical. One or two events—nothing original or especially noteworthy—might be added occasionally, and one or two dropped. Like so many of its counterparts, instead of an annual production, it is an annual re-production.

It survives because there simply isn't anything else going on in that area at that time. There is not much enthusiasm among celebrants, and no one says, "Gosh, I can't wait for next year's festival."

The event just isn't strong enough to magnetize tourists and their dollars. If that festival were rehabilitated, given a spanking new element mix, and promoted with some imaginative marketing know-how, imagine how many more people and dollars it would attract! One TV spokesperson bragged that spectators were "standing four deep in some places" along the parade route. There should have been stacks of 20 or more.

That happening serves as an excellent example and, unfortunately, as a representative of the poorer-quality offerings on the American event scene. Here are some of the reasons events don't reach their potential.

"But We've Always Done It That Way"

The easy way out. "We've done it that way for years, we know it works, so why take a chance on something new and different?" These words are heard often in many corridors of event organiza-tion offices. Similar ones are, "Well, if it's good enough and works well for other cities, then let's do it here," or, "If it ain't broke, don't fix it." Too often, it is "broke" and its people don't even know it.

The festival cited above is several decades old. As noted, it has unfalteringly followed the same format year after year for much of that time, with only inconsequential changes. A few years ago, when there was a top-level reorganization of the festival administrative structure, a highly qualified consultant was contracted to study the event carefully and to give an expert appraisal of it, along with suggestions for its improvement. When told that the festival was stale and badly in need of upgrading, with fresh elements in place of tired ones, the festival board chastised the consultant for "tampering with established tradition that attracts so many people every year." Even though the study explicitly detailed ways to improve the festival significantly with alternatives that would actually reduce production costs, it was immediately shelved. Festival directors went right on with their tattered, frayed, "traditional" event.

Many confuse repetition with tradition. There is a big difference. It's just easier to continue doing things the way they've always been done. When that happens, however, it ensures a ho-hum event year after year.

Lack of Creativity and Innovation

There really isn't a shortage of creativity. There's a surprising amount around. But too little of it is used, especially in the special events field, which by its very nature should epitomize the highest levels of creative application.

In his role as an event marketing consultant, one of the authors of this book has been approached on several occasions by city groups wanting him to help them create a hometown event. "We'd like to do a New Orleans-style Mardi Gras," said one. "A winter carnival like Quebec's," said another.

If an event is to be a tourist attraction—and most of them have that as one of two or three primary objectives—it must be different from and better than others. New Orleans has a well-established claim to hosting North America's premiere Mardi Gras. Quebec City excels in the winter carnival category.

Why attempt what will almost certainly be at best a second-rate copy of someone else's established event? Too many do. How many look-alike summer, winter, music, arts, crafts, ethnic, river, air-show, Oktober, folk, jazz, sports and heritage "fests" are there? Too many, unfortunately.

Some event people feel safe with duplicated theme ideas if the twins are more than 400 miles apart. We totally disagree. If the event is to be a real stand-out in the national—or even regional—event picture, it must be different from and better than others.

Instead of ending a festival with a band or orchestra accompanying fireworks with the "1812 Overture" or "Stars and Stripes Forever," keep the fireworks (always popular), but get different music, stage the pyrotechnical display in a fresh manner, use a different-mix program—make it distinctive! Better yet, come up with a totally unique grand finale, equally or more powerful than the Sousa-Tchaikovsky-fireworks cliché. Knock their socks off!

Someone needs to do for many special event genres, especially festivals, what Walt Disney did for amusement parks.

Uninspired Marketing

An examination of a collection of event publicity packages can be a discouraging effort. Unfortunately, too many of these kits, comprised of lackluster, tired, unprofessional material, are characteristic of the overall marketing program.

A new event, particularly, must be expertly marketed because it doesn't yet have word-of-mouth publicity to help build interest in it. Even established happenings must be the subjects of constantly improved, intensified, imaginative and innovative marketing techniques. (See Chapter Six.)

Poorly Selected and Trained Personnel

Paid staffs or volunteers are too often given jobs for which they are neither well qualified nor properly prepared. (See Chapter Five.)

Too Much, Too Often

Too often events try to offer too much—to the detriment of quality. Chances for success are greatly improved if three stages of really good shows are offered instead of ten that are adequate or less.

Not Enough Money

Underfunding is another big event concern, one that causes some of the problems already noted. If you can't afford an event that, within its own genre, is of Cadillac caliber, then it shouldn't be fielded.

Timing! Timing! Timing!

An even bigger event problem is a matter of time—meaning too little of it in several ways. A premature event usually will not survive; if it does, it will remain scrawny. Allow plenty of time between the feasibility study and the opening of the event. (That study should indicate best scheduling.)

If human power or money is in short supply, consider having the event every other year instead of annually.

Should the community be trying to field more events within a given year than it can support well with financial or human resources, it is probably going to be known for doing a lot of things poorly. Efforts should be made to blend events or to do away with the weakest ones.

What should be obvious seems to elude some event producers. There is one would-be major festival hosted by a large southern city that, despite its sunbelt location, has been heavily rained on in six of the last nine years. You would think timing, i.e. the time of year, would have been reconsidered by now.

And a final time consideration: keep the event compact and offer enough to keep people busy and happily engaged, but don't over-fill the menu. Conversely, don't spread too few activities over too many days.

Poor Physical Conditions

Insufficient parking (the most often heard complaint about American events), lousy pedestrian and motor traffic flow, an inadequate stadium, tattered tents, banged-up buildings, weedy or muddy playing fields, beat up decorations, errant public address systems, litter, bad odors, dirty and unsafe bleachers, burned-out lights or poor lighting in general, soiled uniforms or costumes, malfunctioning scoreboards, confusing—or no—signage...

These are some of the detriments to quality too often found at events. And many of the eyesore problems outlast the event by showing up in news-paper photos, next year's brochure pictures, and television footage. Good housekeeping should be a primary goal for every event.

Bad Skewing

Sometimes planners seem to be holding their events primarily for themselves. It's what they like that counts. This usually results in a poorly attended or complaint-riddled event. A festival billed as a light-hearted, fun-filled offering should not include an outdoor symphony concert featuring works by 17th century Italian composers simply because the chair-person likes that kind of music. Complete objectiv-ity, supported by a well-conducted feasibility study, should determine the event mix.

Clichés

Did you ever wonder whether there was any other way to open a new store ceremonially than having Queen So-and-So, wielding a pair of mam-moth scissors, cut a ribbon while the mayor, store owner, and other officials beam?

Did you ever wish that someone would do something else to break ground for a new project instead of using one or more (gold- or silverpainted) shovels to do so?

Are you convinced that giant bank checks are the only way to illustrate contributions to benefac-tors?

Does every festival have to have a queen and court? (Fortunately for freshness, the feminist move-ment has clamped down on this cliché. Let us hope coronations at events are either abolished entirely or given creative, fresh formats)

In this age of electronic wizardry, must every marathon run end with the winner breaking a rib-bon?

Before these cliches are installed without thinking, think! There is always a new, different, and better way to do it.

FREE VERSUS PAID ADMISSION

The events industry is sharply divided on the question of whether to charge admission to pro-grams or offer them free to the public. Some con-tend that free activities are perceived by the mar-ket to be of inferior quality, so admission is charged. In their words, "If it's worthwhile, you'll charge for it, or people will think it's not any good and they won't go." Others use purchased tickets to control the number of people in attendance. However, dis-tribution of only a certain number of free tickets can also serve that purpose.

Evidence often challenges the premise that free admission hurts attendance. Except for a small percentage of ticketed reserve seats, for example, nearly every major parade magnetizes thousands of spectators. The Pasadena Tournament of Roses Parade draws more than one million spectators, and only a few thousand seats are sold. One free out-door symphony concert in a relatively small Mid-western suburb attracts more than 10,000 people every year. More than 50,000 spectators enjoy a free, day-long West Coast boat race each summer. The free opening ceremonies of the 1987 International Special Olympics Games filled Notre Dame Stadium.

In an age of five- and six-figure sponsorships, which can buy quality happenings, event-goers ex-pect—and find—many free events to be excellent. Conversely, too many paid-admission events are not worth the ticket price.

Generally, free events do work if drawn from "The Three Wells": well-sponsored, well-produced, and well-marketed.

If tickets are sold, be sure the price is equi-table to what's being offered. Booking agents, pro-moters, and entertainers are good sources for rec-ommended price ranges. Noting what the market will bear at comparable local events is helpful. There is no absolute formula for determining admission prices. Just use reason— think carefully before plan-ning a $100-a-plate dinner to benefit a bridge club. Always check local laws governing what percent-ages of income must go to the benefactor.

CHAPTER FIVE

GETTING EVERYTHING DONE

EVENT ORGANIZATION

There are as many event organizational patterns as there are events. In very few cases would identical patterns work for two happenings; there are too many variables: differing objectives, sizes, demographics, staff, volunteers, budgets, etc.

Our general organizational approach is based on a year-long study of events and is a compendium of the best approaches from numerous productions. Because the only "perfect" event management mosaic is the one that works best for a given event, this is offered not as a panacea but as a group of interrelated suggestions from which a workable plan might be devised.

NON-PROFIT AND NON-POLITICIZED

Unless demands dictate otherwise, most events function best if they are supervised by a non-profit corporation. Often, when events are a part of or directly subject to another entity, such as a city department, chamber of commerce, tourism promotion unit, etc., they can suffer from one or more of the following maladies.

Powerful Politics

Changes in parent-entity administrations can result in unwarranted, perhaps harmful, changes in event administrations. Also, those not always best suited for the jobs may receive appointments in return for political favors.

"Fifth-Wheelism "

Too frequently, when an event is assigned to a non-related entity, it is taken on because no one else wants it, no one could decide where else it should go, or "since it was the brain child of that department, let them run it." The truth is, too often events are unwanted responsibilities. When this is the case, minimum effort, time, and funding are given to them; other "more important" and "primary" functions are assigned higher priorities. "We're busy enough already and our budget's too thin without taking on that!" is often thought—and sometimes said—by those in the foster-parent entity. Attitudes, reactions, and results too often mirror that complaint.

Non-Ready-for-Prime-Event Players

Too many people think that to put on an event, all you have to do is do it! This is a danger especially inherent in the practice of assigning a happening to a non-related governing body. The chamber of commerce or the convention and visitors bureau is not necessarily equipped with personnel talented or experienced in event conceptualization and production. If those nonrelated bodies hire someone to run the event, there is a chance for either or both of the above maladies to occur.

Dependency Factor

An event operating on its own prospers through independence. "We're doing it ourselves, and we're proud that we are!" can be a claim that gives spunk to a happening. The role of parent entities should be limited to getting feasibility studies done for proposed events, setting up nonprofit organizations to run them, and giving locally-hosted happenings as much human and monetary support as possible.

A MATTER FOR THE IRS

Many events that rely on contributions, and/or corporate sponsorships, file with the Internal Revenue Service for a "501 (C)(4)" or "501 (C)(3)" status. The 501 (C)(4) category covers such groups as civic leagues, social welfare organizations, and local associations of employees. Their general nature must include promotion of community welfare—charitable, educational or recreational. 501 (C)(3) organizations are required to be educational, scientific, and/or religious in nature. Surprisingly, if considered, many events contain enough activities of an educational nature (i.e., storytelling, in-school programs, educational displays, international exchange, hands-on arts activities, etc.) to qualify under this category.

The difference? 501 (C)(3) organizations are tax deductible, aiding in your search for funding; and also allow you to apply for sales tax exemption, which can be a large line item in an event budget.

Note: *Never assume anything in IRS matters.* Preferably, discuss the status of your event in a one-on-one meeting with your local IRS staff or, if necessary, through correspondence with the Internal Revenue Service in Washington, D.C. Your accountant can assist in this communication and your ultimate application.

THE ORGANIZATION GRID

Both authors have been directly responsible for the feasibility study, initial design, concept implementation, marketing program, sponsorship strategy and operational administration of the Boise River Festival, which began serving the Idaho capital in June 1991. Original attendance was 130,000;

1996's record was more than one million, lifting it to an economic impact level on its community of more than $36 million.

Our studies of hundreds of events, large and small, have significantly enriched our own direct-involvement backgrounds in special events. This fortunate combination enabled us to use the Boise River Festival as a showcase for what we firmly believed to be the best-of-the-best ingredients for a successful event.

With half a decade of proof supporting it (and us), we feel comfortable in using the Boise River Festival as the definitive case study for this book. We do so with the full realization that not all Boise River Festival elements, in their specific form, will work successfully for other events. But we do believe that a great many can be reshaped and/or repositioned to serve as basic event fundamentals.

As is true of most organizational plans, each of the units in the Boise grid falls into one of four independent but strongly interrelated categories: administration—the managers; personnel—securing the right people for the right jobs; operations and production—from idea to reality; and marketing—selling the event.

BOARD OF DIRECTORS

From the very outset of planning, it was determined that the Boise River Festival Board of Directors would be comprised of citizens who have repeatedly demonstrated the highest levels of the following qualities:

- Widely acknowledged expertise in a business, professional, or community service capacity;
- A recognized "influential" with a far-reaching network of contacts;
- Exceptional organizational abilities and administrative talents;
- Eagerness to participate in and support community endeavors;
- Values compatible with those of the community; and
- Sincere desire to serve on the Board and contribute significant talent, time, and effort to the event.

Collectively, a Board should provide all professional and business expertise necessary to ensure an event's operation and success. Therefore, it is suggested that a mixture of talent be represented by the Board of Directors. It will definitely be a working board, although ideally the board should not try to micro-manage the event or take the place of the paid professional staff. A selection of professionals that would be appropriate to almost any board appears in the box below.

BOARD MEMBERS

Board Member 1	The best administrator available, perhaps a Chief Operating Officer or President of a corporation, to serve as Board Chair
Board Member 2	A banker, financier, or any leader in an organization pivoting on money and finance
Board Member 3	A top-level public relations expert, publicist, advertising executive, or marketing practitioner
Board Member 4	A Certified Public Accountant (CPA) or an executive-level corporate comptroller or accountant
Board Member 5	A tourism-promotion executive or anyone in a position of leadership in the travel, hospitality, or leisure-time industries
Board Member 6	An attorney
Board Member 7	A high-ranking representative of city government
Board Members 8+	The top-level position or a representative assigned directly by that person from all major community employers and headquarter companies based in the local market

Note: If a community has only one representative of a major media group (i.e., newspaper, television, radio) then they should be invited (at the highest level — i.e. publisher, president, general manager) to serve on the board. If more than one affiliate exists in any given group, it is safer to invite no one to serve and avoid conflicts of interest claims.

To encourage continuity and year-to-year improvement of the festival, and to discourage staleness, Board members should serve three-year staggered terms in a pattern set by the initial group in a set of bylaws. One common arrangement is to have some members elected to serve one year, some two years, and some three years, all with re-election privileges by majority action of the Board. Any member can be removed at any time by vote of the majority, and any new person can be named to fill vacancies by like action. Board members should serve without compensation, but authorized expenses should be reimbursed. The total number of board members should not be unmanageable and should preferably be uneven in number to assure a tie-breaker vote if ever necessary.

Boise board members serve as executive liaisons between the chairperson(s) of operating committees and the board. This keeps the board involved in the actual operations of the Festival. It is helpful to match board members with committees that make the best use of their expertise, where possible. All members serve the Board as advisors on matters involving their specialties.

COMMITTEE STRUCTURES AND RELATIONSHIPS

Again, we will call on the Boise River Festival for a four-day event to illustrate an effective committee grid and the interrelationships among those groups. Of course, this organizational layout may not be suitable in its entirety for other events, but hopefully it will spur approaches that will tighten and strengthen committee functions and improve inter-committee harmony.

In the now more mature Boise plan, there are 30+ operating committees covering different functions. Because you will determine many of your own needs as your event grows and develops, we have expanded on some of the more basic/foundation committees below. Following these is a list to spur other possibilities and considerations as appropriate or required. You may find that for your own event it makes more sense to combine functions, lowering the number of committees, at least initially. The main goal is to allow each committee to focus its efforts on a specific area, ensuring quality results.

If help or support is needed (i.e., the entertainment committee needs a van to pick up entertainers), other committees are called on to provide assistance (in this case, the transportation committee would provide the requested van).

Except for the Event Production Committee, the overall managing group of the event, committees are not listed in order of importance. Committees may also be broken into appropriate subcommittees to better maximize efficiency and work load. *Note:* Committee chairs and members are generally volunteers and should serve without compensation, but authorized expenses should be reimbursed.

Note: We emphasize here again that the following committees and their individual structures are those that have evolved so productively over the years specifically in the development of the Boise River Festival. Committees and optional structures presented in the companion book, *Making Special Events Fit in the 21st Century,* are generic representations, from which individual events may borrow and adapt concepts and structures more suited to their own profiles.

EVENT PRODUCTION COMMITTEE

Membership: Executive Director/President serves as Committee Chairperson; membership is comprised of the other committee chairpersons and the paid event staff.

General Description: This is the front-line supervising body. Chairpersons of all other committees are members of this group, which is broadly responsible for quality control of all event components, planning, implementation, results reporting, etc.

Specific Responsibilities:
- Supervise annual budget development and event content for Board approval;
- Call general meetings of all committee chairpersons;
- Call meetings of groups of committees;
- Assign committee responsibilities;
- Coordinate interrelated activities and communication between committees;

- Ensure that all event elements meet or surpass established quality-control criteria;
- Handle all crises, sensitive, or potentially troublesome matters;
- Carefully select and supervise coordinators assigned to directly supervise segments of the event; and
- Evaluate event operations and suggest operational changes.

ACCOUNTING COMMITTEE

General Description: Monetary control and reporting procedures are the important and sole assignment of this committee.

Specific Responsibilities:
- Establish and stringently enforce tight monetary controls over every committee, function, and the event in general;
- Prepare financial statements and deliver them regularly to the Board of Directors and Event Production Committee; and
- Prepare all required tax forms and other legally required reports.

COMMUNICATIONS COMMITTEE

General Description: Constant communication is an important key to a successful event and it is the responsibility of the Communications Committee to provide the necessary communication links between staff, committees and emergency personnel to ensure that success throughout the event.

Specific Responsibilities:
- Identify committee and staff needs for radios and cellular telephones and secure the same;
- Assignment and training on all radios and cellular telephones to event staff;
- Maintain an event communications center and battery recharge/replacement function on-site during the event; and
- Post-event collection and return of all radios and cellular telephones.

DECORATIONS COMMITTEE

General Description: This group is responsible for "getting the house ready for company and a celebration." Quality and good taste are its goals, along with creating THE LOOK and atmosphere of the overall event.

Specific Responsibilities:
- Arrange for the event posters, banners, street decorations, etc. to be used throughout the city;
- Arrange for the production of decorative items and the placement of street and other suspended decorations requiring crews for installation;
- Arrange with merchants and other venues for the display of decorations;
- Provide advice, suggestions, and encouragement for individualized custom displays and decorations in commercial and other public establishments;
- Control use of all decorations; and
- Provide for immediate and proper dismantling and storage of all decorations following the event.

ENTERTAINMENT COMMITTEE

General Description: This unit is responsible for the event's entertainment programming, a primary pivot of most events. Its importance cannot be overstated.

Specific Responsibilities:
- Assure maximum quality of all entertainment;
- Research, audition, select, prepare and negotiate contracts when necessary, and credential all performing groups and individuals appearing under the auspices of the event;
- Set and enforce appearance and performance content codes for all entertainers;
- Work with the Facilities, Equipment, and Supplies Committee to determine and arrange for all rental, purchase, installation, and operation of equipment and facilities, including platforms, stages, sound systems, lighting, sets, etc., needed for entertainment purposes;
- Cooperate with the Marketing Committee in satisfying such needs as performer availability for interviews, photos, media appearances, and advertising requirements;
- Advise the Transportation Committee on special needs in the movement of performers and support items; and
- Work with appropriate committees to meet performer contract rider obligations.

FACILITIES, EQUIPMENT AND SUPPLIES COMMITTEE

General Description: In effect, this is the "purchasing agent" for the event and is its sole supplier. By vesting purchasing power as much as possible in this one unit, volume cost savings can be effected, duplication can be avoided, and use-control can be better assured.

Specific Responsibilities:
- Set up procedures for all committees to order all facilities, equipment, and supplies;
- Establish an efficient system of use-control for all such items;
- Solicit items as in-kind contributions from potential sponsors;
- Arrange for all purchases, leases and rentals, negotiating for best prices, delivery arrangements, etc.;
- Maintain a carefully controlled distribution system for supplies;
- Work with the Transportation Committee to arrange for items to be transported as needed, such as tents, stages and platforms, chairs, food service support equipment, sound systems, office equipment and supplies, signs and banners, all construction needs, lighting, etc.;
- Serve as quality control relative to the appearance of all structural entities; and
- Negotiate construction crews with suppliers where needed.

MAINTENANCE COMMITTEE

General Description: Cleanliness is especially equal to Godliness in the special events realm. The importance of a well-policed host area cannot be emphasized too often, and neither can the importance of this committee. Anything related to cleanliness, sanitation, facilities grooming, etc., are within the jurisdiction of this unit.

Specific Responsibilities:
- Guarantee ecological and environmental integrity in all event activities;
- Ensure a clutter-free condition for all event sites at all times;
- Order and place portable public restrooms through the Facilities, Equipment and Supply Committee, and ensure that these facilities are in locations easily accessible to the public but removed from incompatible situations, such as food serving and consumption areas;
- Arrange for frequent collection and removal of refuse from all areas;
- Ensure odor control; and
- Serve as quality control for the appearance of all areas.

MARKETING COMMITTEE

General Description: Unless an event is effectively and repeatedly promoted, it is doomed to failure. It is up to this unit first to "sell" the event to every person in its market area and then to reach a steadily-expanded market zone. Because of monetary restrictions, paid advertising is likely to be limited; therefore, emphasis should be placed on non-paid publicity to carry the event campaign to the public.

Specific Responsibilities:
- Design a detailed, thorough, highly imaginative marketing plan, that takes advantage of every "natural" and "created" opportunity during the year to focus public attention throughout the market area on the event;
- Build into that plan strong interplays and support efforts among all elements of marketing —advertising, publicity, public relations, and promotions;
- Compile and maintain completely updated name and address files on best media contacts;
- Place strict controls over all expenditures;
- Coordinate and oversee general and economic impact surveys of event attendees and compile results following the event; Develop and maintain the highest quality media relations possible; and

- Maintain complete press/video files of event coverage.

RISK MANAGEMENT COMMITTEE

General Description: Event insurers encourage this type of committee, to help reduce and eliminate the potential for accidents and injuries during your event.

Specific Responsibilities:
- Create and provide guidelines to all event committees on how to reduce the risk of accidents;
- Work with the Visitor Services Committee to provide for a quick response to any accident, injuries, or illnesses on-site during the event;
- Create and plan for the distribution and collection of accident report forms to attendees, volunteers, and emergency support agencies;
- Walk through the event to identify any risky situations that have not been caught and arrange for their correction; and
- Maintain constant communications with the event insurer to stay up to date on current insurance concerns and issues, event policies, and any new event programs/activities that may effect insurance coverage/protection.

SECURITY COMMITTEE

General Description: The larger the event, the greater the need for volunteer security. This important committee acts as additional eyes and ears for law enforcement agencies in providing a safe environment for attendees and also plays a critical role in guarding the plethora of equipment, props, vehicles, event sites, facilities, etc. against theft and/or vandalism.

Specific Responsibilities:
- Determine security needs of all event committees and activities and provide volunteer security for same;
- Properly train all security volunteers in how to deal with specific situations without putting themselves in a dangerous situation;
- Develop a communications and support plan with local law enforcement agencies; and

Working with the Visitor Services, Risk Management and Marketing Committees, local law enforcement and emergency agencies, and the event Executive Director/President, create and distribute an event emergency and communications plan to be followed in the event of a major emergency.

SIGNAGE AND BANNERS COMMITTEE

General Description: Who, what, when, where, why and how are all answered for event attendees and volunteers through on-site signage and banners. This enormous amount of information must be created in an attractive, cost effective and high quality manner. This is the job of the Signage and Banners Committee.

Specific Responsibilities:
- Work with all committees (especially Sponsor Services, Visitor Services, and Entertainment) to determine appropriate needs for signage and banners, including but not limited to, sponsor banners, directional and information signs, vehicle signage, and entertainment/stage schedules;
- Create new, innovative, attractive and cost effective alternatives to meet those needs and maintain quality control of the same throughout the event grounds and venues;
- Arrange for the proper and attractive hanging and distribution of all signage and banners at appropriate times and locations; and
- Arrange for the quick collection, inventory, clean-up, repair and proper storage of all signage and banners, to insure multiple years of use.

TRANSPORTATION COMMITTEE

General Description: There is an axiom in the events industry which, unfortunately, is too true too often: if anything goes wrong in a special event, it will be the transportation. For some reason, too many gatherings find it difficult to schedule the right transportation at the right times. This committee must foresee and satisfy every kind of transportation need for event working units as well as for celebrants.

Specific Responsibilities:
- Determine all transportation needs of celebrants;
- Arrange for donated transportation or negotiate best deal for such;
- Select best routes and most suitable stops for shuttle buses, and arrange with Signage and Banners Committee for appropriate signage at those stops;
- Working with the Sponsorship and the Marketing Committees, determine what signage is needed for any vehicles (examples: sponsorship credit banner for shuttle buses; event promotion signs on city buses), and arrange with the Signage and Banners Committee for such;
- Determine the part private transportation— event fleet automobiles, recreational vehicles, bicycles, cabs, city buses, etc.—will play in the event, and make adequate arrangements for such, working closely with appropriate agencies and sponsors; and
- Elicit from all other committees their transportation needs—trucks, golf carts, bicycles, passenger vehicles, VIP limos, etc. — and meet those needs.

VENDOR COMMITTEE

General Description: Any activity involving food, beverages, and souvenir sales, whether purchased or consumed as part of the event, is included in this committee's duties.

Specific Responsibilities:
- Seek, screen, approve, and certify all official vendors participating in any direct way in the event;
- Serve as quality control for all beverage, food, merchandise, and vendor activities;
- Reach retail price agreements with all sellers;
- Determine financial arrangements (registration fees, space rental sums, etc.) for vendors,
- Establish secure and efficient systems for collecting all monies and script and for depositing those funds with Accounting Committee representatives;

- Work with the Maintenance Committee and Health Department to ensure that all food service areas are always in the best order; and
- Establish and strictly enforce dress and appearance codes for all vendor personnel/booths.

VISITOR SERVICES COMMITTEE

General Description: Making your "guests" feel at home is the responsibility of this important committee. From directions to first aid to lost kids, your visitors will appreciate the royal treatment and return year after year.

Specific Responsibilities:
- Identify programs that will directly impact event-goers and their potential needs while attending your activities. These may include information, first aid, lost kids, lost and found, telephones, ATM machines, handicapped access, schedule changes, ride home programs (if alcohol is served), parking, shuttle stops and more;
- Create programs and plans to efficiently and cost-effectively meet those needs; and
- Work with the Marketing Committee to get information out to the general public through the media before arriving at your event.

VOLUNTEER RESOURCES COMMITTEE

General Description: Getting The Right People in The Right Jobs—that is the goal of this unit. Proper staffing is one of two absolute requirements of an event, the other being adequate funding.

Specific Responsibilities:
- Work with all committees to determine person power needs through Volunteer Resources-designed procedures;
- Spearhead volunteer enlistment campaigns;
- Assign volunteers to committees;
- Troubleshoot any personnel difficulties;
- Work with organized labor if the need should arise;
- Arrange for and assign any purchased labor; and

- Oversee training and motivational programs for all volunteers, ensuring a high annual retention rate.

Note: The following list includes functions that may be combined with an existing committee, divided out as a sub-committee of another function, or as growth and workload may dictate, added on or divided out as committees of their own. You will, without doubt, discover still others that make sense for your own event.

- ACCESS CONTROL—to parking and special VIP hospitality areas, ticketed seating areas and backstage control
- CHILDREN'S ACTIVITIES—self-explanatory grouping of activities
- ENVIRONMENTAL PRE-CAUTIONS & PROTECTION—self-explanatory grouping of activities, especially important in today's event market
- INDEPENDENT FUND RAISING EFFORTS/ACTIVITIES NOT AFFILIATED WITH SPONSORSHIP
- HEALTH SERVICES—first aid, paramedics, ambulance, etc.
- INVENTORY CONTROL—the construction, repair, maintenance, storage and control of all event-owned assets
- MERCHANDISE SALES—self-explanatory
- MEDIA RELATIONS—self-explanatory
- PARADES AND/OR OTHER MAJOR EVENTS which entail substantial details and workload, may need to operate as committees on their own
- PERIMETERS—pre-sets and controls boundaries for events, venues, parades, fireworks, talent, and more, using barricades, rope, fencing, flags, etc.
- PRIZES & AWARDS—secures prizes and awards for all event contests, participants, sponsors, volunteers, etc., as needed
- SPORTING ACTIVITIES—self-explanatory grouping of activities
- TECHNICAL SUPPORT—works with entertainment committee to provide and meet all needs by on-stage performers
- TELEVISION COVERAGE—as necessary, if events are televised at length
- TRAFFIC CONTROL—working with local police to create necessary road closures and traffic control

PAID STAFF

Some very polished, successful events operate without any paid staff whatsoever, with a chairperson and volunteer administrators being named for varying lengths of service. When budgets permit, however, it is better to have at least one permanent full-time, paid professional—usually titled "Executive Director" or "President"—to head up the effort. This provides consistency, continuity, and know-how. Once budgets grow, one after another of the following professionals should be hired, usually in this order:

1. *Sponsorship solicitation manager,* if the event depends heavily on contributed funding;

2. *Marketing manager,* an expert in publicity, promotions, and advertising;

3. *Entertainment or sports event manager;*

4. *Assistant to the Executive Director,* specializing in budget and finance;

5. *Assistant sponsorship solicitation manager;*

6. *Assistant marketing manager,* a specialist in publicity;

7. *Assistant entertainment or sports event manager;* and

8. *Volunteer resources manager*—coordinator of volunteer solicitation, training, and assignments.

THE IDEAL EXECUTIVE DIRECTOR

In considering the type of person who should serve in this crucial position, it is extremely important to caution that this individual should not be inflexibly tied to traditional, "we've always done it that way" event-management practices. The administrator must be an innovator who is willing to try new approaches and apply creative solutions to all kinds of challenges.

The person holding this position may or may not have had event administrative experience. Having such a background is a plus, all other assets being equal. But it need not be a required absolute. In designing the Boise Festival Master Plan, its author described essential qualifications for the executive director. These qualifications appear in the box below.

Executive Director Qualifications

1. He/she must be, first and foremost, a world-class administrator, an organizer and a doer of the first order. This is someone who gets things done.
2. His/her people skills must be the best. The abilities to inspire and motivate associates and to function well with the Board of Directors are essential.
3. The successful candidate should be able to demonstrate through past accomplishments the highest degree of creativity, in terms of both imaginative concepts and problem solving.
4. A reasonably strong personality is an essential endowment. The executive director should be able to insist on—and get—the highest caliber of performance from all associated with the event, even volunteers. He/she will be a stern and effective chief of quality control for the entire happening.
5. He/she must be able to say—and stay with—no, when it would be much easier to say yes, and vice versa.

EXECUTIVE DIRECTOR COMPENSATION

A sponsorship, per se, is generally not suitable to support a hired official. However, some events have found that good corporate citizen companies in their areas may either pay for that executive or, in essence, "give" that executive, with all costs paid, to an event.

In terms of salary, it is not possible to give specific figures here. The income level depends on the cost of living in a given locale, and the size, longevity, history, and means of support of the event.

In 1995 and on an every-other-year basis, the International Festivals & Events Association publishes a survey of executive and staff compensations and other pertinent event information affecting this area. It would benefit event boards or executives to contact the IFEA and obtain a copy to use as a guide for determining reasonable salary levels. (For the IFEA address, **see page 72**).

WORKING EFFECTIVELY WITH VOLUNTEERS

Volunteers are the backbone of most events. Volunteers can augment your event staff; expand your outreach and support; provide expertise and direction; maximize resources and minimize expenses; and involve the community in a community event. Yet we have found that too few events have truly effective training or recruiting programs for these important helpers.

The best happenings have volunteers who are:

- brought into the event picture early enough to contribute to its planning and get a feel for its basics;
- enthusiastic because event management has created an atmosphere of genuine enthusiasm that is highly contagious;
- part of a team, in every meaning of the phrase, feeling and being truly important;
- worked with, not worked over; and thoroughly prepared to carry out their event responsibilities.

Event management really begins with volunteer selection. Therefore, training and working effectively with volunteers should be among the highest priorities of the event management. Too often, a general call goes out for help and the various respondents are somewhat randomly assigned to jobs, with a few words of instruction about their duties.

The ideal recruitment process with the highest potential for success is much more systematic. Assuming that the event is not-for-profit, it generally reflects the following pattern.

As in well-run commercial enterprises, well-run events begin with management making up a list of absolutely essential jobs, providing for every need but including no unnecessary or contingency positions.

As noted with the organization outlined for the Boise River Festival, the essentials are generally in the areas identified under the committee structures and relationships section of this chapter.

When the list is complete, a concise job description should be prepared for each key position, and should indicate the preferred background for the person filling the job. It is rare that someone will perfectly fit the "Preferred Background" description; however, it will serve as an excellent guideline in helping to find the nearest thing to a perfect fit. An event manager and/or a "borrowed" expert in human resources should help supervise the job description preparations.

An example of an event job description appears in the box on the next page.

With all job descriptions combining to become an Event Operations Staffing Manual, management should note the most likely places to recruit the right volunteer for each position. For the Publicity Manager in our example, sources might include local news media, public relations agencies, membership rosters of such professional organizations as the Public Relations Society of America, newspaper business pages or public relations columns.

Assertiveness is called for. Pick up the phone and call sources to determine whether they can provide names of potential volunteers—and call prospective volunteers directly. If another current volunteer knows the potential candidate directly, include them in the process. Since the event is non-profit and is likely serving some worthy need, even if it's just a festival to provide fun and entertainment, play heavily on the good citizenship role volunteers will play; the tremendous network of other community volunteers already involved; the fun, experience, and positive working atmosphere offered by the event; and the high value placed on their involvement.

When all jobs are filled, call a general meeting of all key volunteers (committee chairs). The timing of this gathering rests on the size of the event and the number of volunteers. Generally, this first meeting should take place about six to eight months prior to the first day of the event, for small to medium size events, and ten to twelve months prior to a large event.

This gathering should offer everyone a complete overview of the event, answering all questions vital to every volunteer—the organization and in-

EVENT JOB DESCRIPTION

Committee: Marketing
Position: Publicity Manager
Estimated Time Commitment: Minimal—July to Dec., Extensive—Jan. to June
Supervisor: Chairperson, Marketing Committee
Preferred Background: Editorial assistant, news writer or editor, professional public relations practitioner, free-lance writer with proven publication record, or eduator in journalism or public relations. Three or more years' experience. Previous event experience a plus but not required.

Responsibilities:

1. Prepare and submit to the marketing Chairperson and effective publicity strategy for the event, outlining plans and timing, with periodic updates as needed.
2. Create, prepare, and submit professional quality material for television, radio, newspaper, magazine, printed program, and other media in accordance with the publicity strategy.
3. Establish and maintain effective contacts with all appropriate news media representatives.
4. Respond quickly and effectively to all media inquiries.
5. Initiate or respond to requests for, plan, and conduct interviews, photo opportunities, and media conferences.
6. Recruit, train, and manage volunteer Media Hosts to accompany and assist visiting media before, during and immediately following the event.
7. Provide media training for appropriate event officials who may serve as media spokesperson.
8. Arrange for, edit, and supervise all photography designed for media use.
9. Set up, manage, and maintain the official event Media Headquarters.
10. Collect and organize effectively all press clippings radio tapes and television clips, and combine them into a final Publicity Report due to the Marketing Committee Chairperson within one month following the final day of the event.

terrelationships among its operating units, budgets, sponsor needs, etc.

Immediately afterwards, the individual committees should hold their first meetings with their hand-selected member volunteers. It is here that the event actually starts to become a reality.

Committee meetings will vary broadly in their timing, format, and content. Some committees feel the pressure of their workload much earlier than others and some may not get fully involved until two or three months prior to the event.

The Event Production Committee, which should meet monthly beginning as early as a year prior to the event, serves the purpose of keeping all committees on track with one another.

The "cast of thousands", volunteers who have agreed to fill basic event duties such as trash pickup, soft drink sales, etc., will not need to come into the picture until a few weeks prior to the event, but should receive the same quality training and appreciation, usually overseen by individual committee chairs.

The moment event facilities are in place, every committee should conduct its own on-site walkthrough so that each person knows precisely what to do, where and when, and for good measure, what others will be doing that might influence his or her own responsibilities. The walk-through is absolutely essential and should follow a final in-depth Event Production Committee meeting to discuss last-minute concerns and updates.

Following the event, volunteers should be asked to fill out formal evaluation forms regarding their experience, with suggestions for improvement. Retention of these valuable resources depends on listening to and responding to their needs and input.

For more detailed recommendations and strategies for effectively working with volunteers, we recommend the following books:

Managing Volunteers by the International Festivals & Events Association

The Effective Management of Volunteer Programs by Marcene Wilson

Essential Volunteer Management by Steve McCurley and Rick Lynch

THE SPECIAL EVENT "IMPLEVENTER"

THE IDEAL EVENT ORGANIZATION

As discussed earlier in this book, the ideal organization for the implementation of most events has four strongly interrelated, basic units. These units can be handled by four teams. In some instances, especially in the case of a small event, duties of more than one team might be handled by a single department. Although the teams may be labeled differently from organization to organization, the quartet of essential functions remains the same. A description of these teams and their functions follows.

Administrative Team

These people are the "headquarters staff." They're the managers, and their leader is the top gun of the entire event.

Personnel Team

It's up to this group's members to get the right people fitted into the right jobs, provide orientation and training for newcomers, and to handle all other personnel matters. In industry, Human Resources is the label used.

Operations Team

These are the doers! They are the ones who make the event and its location work together.

Marketing Team

Meet the sales staff. These men and women promote the event—to the public, sponsors, media, etc.—either directly through ticket sales and sponsorship solicitation or indirectly with advertising and publicity.

NOTES ABOUT THE "IMPLEVENTER"

The Impleventer, a master, all-purpose event implementation check list, is designed to be a model for copying and can be used as is or tailored specifically to an event. If the following form is used, line items applicable to the given event can be checked in the blank at the left of each, and the names of the persons assigned to each task can be listed to the right along with established deadlines for the accomplishment of each item.

Everyone working on an event should be easy to reach, and this is especially true for those in management positions. The Impleventer leads off with an example of the kind of contact sheet that satisfies this need. The "Other" under "Telephones" should include the numbers of weekend retreat locations, second offices, friends or relatives with whom that person is in frequent contact, car phones and so on.

At one time or another, the services of one or more attorneys will probably be needed. Whenever possible, the same lawyer should be used for all event needs. However, in the case of very large endeavors, there may be a need for legal specialists. These specialists might include attorneys familiar with artist contracts, others more expert in venue agreements, etc.

Broadly speaking, the Operations Team is an order-taker for all units' support needs such as those related to the physical plant, site, or facilities accommodating the event. Ideally, working closely with the Personnel Team, the Operations Team will also be charged with helping to secure people to run the event in support roles.

By being the primary recruiting force, the Personnel Team can efficiently coordinate all searches of temporary-help providers, volunteer groups, college job-placement offices, and employment agencies. The only exceptions are highly specialized personnel, best selected by the teams with whom they will work, such as electricians, set designers and float builders for Operations, and publicists and advertising people for Marketing. In these areas, Personnel should work closely with the ap-propriate teams to secure the best possible individuals for the job.

As closely as possible, Impleventer items have been arranged in chronological progression. However, many of the assignments—even those within a Team—must be accomplished virtually simultaneously. Examples: Contracts may have to be negotiated within a very short period of time, and perhaps several will be signed in a single day. Also, media preparations within Marketing may often have to be done by several people at the same time. Therefore, deadlines frequently should be the same for more than two or three items.

Note: Although the Impleventer was used in the crafting of the previously discussed Boise Master Plan, the format and terminology were changed in the interest of providing a more effective verbal, as well as written, presentation. Such changes in this instrument, including moving about responsibilities from one team to another, make it a flexible guideline.

The Special Event
"Impleventer"

Event_____

Event Date (s) _____

Location (s) _____

***

Assignments:

Senior General Coordinator
and Coordinator of Administrative team _____

    Address _____

    Telephones: Office _____

                   Home _____

                   Other _____

Personnel Team Coordinator _____

    Address _____

    Telephones: Office _____

                   Home _____

                   Other _____

Operations Team Coordinator _____

    Address _____

    Telephones: Office _____

                   Home _____

                   Other _____

Marketing Team Coordinator

    Address _____

    Telephones: Office _____

                   Home _____

                   Other _____

Other _____

    Address _____

    Telephones: Office _____

                   Home _____

                   Other _____

***

Administrative Team

DUTIES OF SENIOR GENERAL COORDINATOR AND ADMINISTRATIVE TEAM STAFF

RESPONSIBILITY	ASSIGNED TO	DEADLINE
Schedule and conduct staff meetings	_____	_____
Select coordinators of event teams	_____	_____
VIP and sponsor relations	_____	_____
Approve all plans created by or for all event teams	_____	_____
Prepare overall periodic reports to sponsors and others	_____	_____
Establish and supervise budgets	_____	_____
Handle emergencies, problems and disputes	_____	_____
Choose and make arrangements for rain (back-up) date with all event teams	_____	_____
Approve, sign all contracts	_____	_____

Notes, Special Instructions

_____

_____

_____

Personnel Team
(May have major units for entertainment, sports, etc.)

CONTRACT DEVELOPMENT AND NEGOTIATIONS   ASSIGNED TO

_____

DEADLINE

____Select and meet with legal counsel   _____
(May be shared with other teams)

____Complete basic contract preparations   _____

____Negotiate contracts with:

____Booking agents or show producers   _____

____Artists or participants   _____

_____ Specialized paid support staff
(electricians, float builders, stage crews, etc.)   _____

TALENT OR PARTICIPANT SEARCH, AUDITION
OR ENLISTMENT
                                                        ASSIGNED TO

_____

DEADLINE

____Determine best means of selecting talent/participants   _____

____Choose booking agent or other source   _____

____Determine number needed for stage crew, on-site
talent/participant assistance, etc. (Notify Operations)   _____

____Set dates and times for briefings, rehearsals,
auditions or meetings (Notify Operations,
Marketing). Then: _____

____Arrange location(s) with Operations

____Arrange for all on-site facility needs
with Operations   _____

____Coordinate media, publicity, photo needs with
Marketing   _____

____Arrange for special needs—sound, lights, set,
costumes, accompanist, sports equipment, etc.   _____

_____Initial notification of staff, talent/participants
of times, dates, locations

_____

_____Set briefing (time and location) for staff assistants

_____

_____Final reminder of time and place to staff,
talent/participants, Operations, Marketing

_____

_____Report results to Administration

_____

COORDINATION WITH OPERATIONS UNIT

ASSIGNED TO

_____

DEADLINE

Notify Operations Unit of:

_____

_____Total long distance travel needs for pre-, during-,
and post-event periods

_____

_____Participant-related ground transportation needs
and arrange driver briefings

_____

_____On-site furnishing needs—seating arrangements,
telephones, off-stage talent requirements, etc.

_____

_____Participant-related security needs

_____

_____On-stage talent requirements
(lighting, sound, props, etc.)

_____

COORDINATION WITH MARKETING UNIT

ASSIGNED TO

_____

DEADLINE

Set times, dates, locations for:

_____Publicity still photos and videos

_____

_____Media interviews

_____

_____VIP and sponsor tie-ins—receptions, cast parties, etc.

_____

_____Any special advertising needs

_____

____Outside promotional appearances   _____

____Media coverage of pre-event activities and event itself

STAFF ENLISTMENT AND TRAINING

ASSIGNED TO

_____

Determine non-talent/participant personnel requirements, sources for each, and set up training and briefing time-tables for each. (Categories may be employees or volunteers or both)

DEADLINE

_____

CATEGORY	NUMBER
____Ticket sellers	_____
____Ticket takers	_____
____Ride operators	_____
____Attractions operators	_____
____Judges, umpires, referees	_____
____Stage or field production crews	_____
____Ushers	_____
____Souvenir sales	_____
____Food sellers	_____
____Telephone personnel	_____
____Messengers	_____
____Walkie-talkie and/or radio operators	_____
____Drivers	_____
____Emergency/first-aid	_____
____Maintenance	_____
____Janitorial	_____
____Security personnel	_____
____"Gofers"	_____
____Other	_____

Notes, Special Instructions

_____

_____

_____

Operations Team

CONTRACT DEVELOPMENT AND NEGOTIATIONS

ASSIGNED TO

_____

DEADLINE

_____Select and meet with legal counsel
(May be shared with other teams)

_____

_____Complete basic contract preparations

_____

Negotiate contracts with:
    _____Venues and facilities for staging event

_____

    _____Vendors of food, souvenirs, etc.

_____

    _____Outside security agency

_____

    _____Paid judges, umpires, referees

_____

    _____Hall or stadium furnishers—seats,
    service counters, etc.

_____

    _____Communications companies for telephones,
    walkie-talkies, etc.

_____

    _____Lodging units for teams, participants,
    artists, staff, etc.

_____

    _____Vehicle purchase, lease or rental companies

_____

    _____Paid staff members and crews

_____

    _____Maintenance and clean-up personnel

_____

    _____Trash removal and disposal company

_____

    _____Emergency and first-aid staffs

_____

    _____Labor unions

_____

    _____Supplier (s) of unskilled labor

_____

    _____Insurance companies

_____

    _____Specialized Equipment

_____

    _____Construction

_____

PERMITS, CERTIFICATES AND INSPECTIONS

ASSIGNED TO

_____

Deadline

_____ City special event permits   _____

_____ Law enforcement agencies   _____

_____ Highway and traffic-control authorities   _____

_____ Fire Departments   _____

_____ Parks/Facilities use   _____

_____ Public safety organizations   _____

_____ Environmental-control agencies   _____

_____ Water-control units (such as U.S. Coast   _____
        Guard, Corps of Engineers, etc.)

_____ Aviation administrative agencies (use of   _____
        airplanes, hot-air balloons, etc.)

_____ Health Department   _____

_____ Insurance (including that provided by   _____
        and to the event)

SPECIAL REQUIREMENTS

ASSIGNED TO

_____

DEADLINE

_____Facility-related sponsor needs   _____
(information from marketing)

_____Arrangements for product sampling or sales   _____

_____Special facility needs for talent, staff or participants   _____

_____Planned ticket distribution and collection   _____

_____Plan for returning of site to prior state

Notes, Special Instructions

_____

_____

Marketing Team

SPONSORSHIPS

ASSIGNED TO

_____

DEADLINE

Determine sponsorship opportunities

_____

Research/develop sponsorship sales strategy
and candidate lists

_____

Prepare sponsorship proposals

_____

Make appointments with sponsor candidates

_____

Sponsorship sales meetings

_____

Last date for sponsor decisions

_____

Report results to all event teams

_____

Negotiate sponsorship contracts

_____

Plan sponsor relations during event

_____

Report outcome of event to sponsors

_____

Sponsor thank you letters/gifts

_____

CONTRACT DEVELOPMENT AND NEGOTIATIONS

ASSIGNED TO

_____

DEADLINE

____Select and meet with legal counsel (May be shared
with other teams)

_____

____Complete basic contract preparations

_____

Negotiate contracts with:

____PR/publicity agency

_____

____Advertising agency

_____

____Still photographer

_____

____Video production company

_____

____Press clippings service   _____

____Television monitoring service   _____

____Television, radio sponsors   _____

____Cablevision/Network representatives   _____

____Satellite transmission services   _____

____Graphic design/production companies   _____

____Sponsors of event   _____

PUBLICITY

ASSIGNED TO

_____

DEADLINE

____Prepare fully detailed, written strategy with
publicity agency   _____

____Brief sponsors and all members of event teams on
plan; also include photographers and video personnel   _____

____Determine special media needs required for
pre-, during-, and post-event periods; notify
appropriate teams   _____

____Talent/participant involvements   _____

____Media meals and receptions   _____

____"Quiet room" for interviews*   _____

____Interview times and locations*   _____

____Rehearsal coverage plans*   _____

____Special backdrops for video, still photo purposes*   _____

____Special lighting*   _____

____Sound-system tie-ins*   _____

____Periodic on-site media briefing plans*   _____

____Times and locations of photo sessions *   _____

____Day-of-event detailed timetable*   _____

____Preferential seating for media*   _____

____Design, supervise prize or trophy award ceremonies   _____

____Collect all media results, devise measurement
formula and report findings periodically to all
event teams   _____

*Notify or in cooperation with Operations

ADVERTISING

ASSIGNED TO

_____

DEADLINE

____Prepare written strategy with advertising agency   _____

____Brief sponsors and all members of event teams
on plan   _____

____Coordinate photo and video sessions with
Operations Team   _____

____Develop logo, copylines of event   _____

PROMOTIONS

ASSIGNED TO

_____

DEADLINE

____Help develop and coordinate cross-promotion
opportunities for event sponsors   _____

____Develop proposals for possible tie-ins with
non-sponsorship products or services   _____

____Contact all appropriate promotion candidate
groups (including TV, radio stations,
newspapers, magazines, etc.)   _____

____Brief all event teams on plans   _____

GRAPHICS

ASSIGNED TO

_____

DEADLINE

____Determine graphics needs, complete designs
and order:

_____

    ____Business stationery
    Quantity _____

_____

    ____Media release letterhead
    Quantity _____

_____

    ____Invitations—number_____

_____

    ____Tickets— number _____

_____

    ____Brochures, pamphlets, other handouts
    Quantity _____

_____

    ____Advance promotional signs
    Size _____Number _____
    Size _____Number _____
    Size _____Number _____

_____

    ____Posters
    Number _____

_____

    ____Banners

_____

    Size _____Number _____
    Copy _____

    Size _____Number _____
    Copy _____

    Size _____Number _____
    Copy _____

    ____Printed programs or event schedules
    Quantity _____

_____

    ____Facility and crowd-directions signs

_____

    Size _____Number _____
    Copy _____

    Size _____Number _____
    Copy _____

Size _____ Number _____
Copy _____

_____ Other _____   _____

Notes, Special Instructions

_____

_____

_____

━ CHAPTER SIX ━

TELL 'EM ABOUT IT!

CREATIVE MARKETING— ONE OF THE GREATEST NEEDS

A successful event has three indispensable ingredients: good planning, good implementation, and good marketing. Some say good marketing is the most important ingredient and argue that the best event in the world doesn't exist unless it draws enough people. And people have to know an event is happening to be there. They must also be convinced to spend their time and money on the event rather than on other opportunities.

All of the expectations, projections, and hopes represented in these pages will be neutralized unless the event, regardless of its size, is properly marketed. This is particularly important if the happening is new. Word-of-mouth is a big attendance accelerator once an event has some history, but for both infant and mature events an effective marketing strategy is essential. The outline of such a strategy follows.

PUBLICITY AND ADVERTISING

In the interest of clarity and understanding, let's review two terms that were introduced earlier. Recall that publicity is the process of obtaining free time or space in the communications media. Advertising, by contrast, is the process of purchasing time or space in the communications media.

PUBLICITY IN TOURISM FEEDER AREAS

Prohibitive costs of advertising usually restrict the use of that option in the marketing mix of a fund-limited event. Therefore, every publicity technique and opportunity must be utilized. That is not to say that publicity can take the place of advertising. Each has its own role, its own strengths, its own weaknesses. However, in the absence of enough money to support an adequate advertising program, publicity must be utilized to its fullest potential.

Although they may be eager to reach certain special interest groups, such as tennis fans or golf buffs, event publicists most often aim their major thrusts at two much broader targets: local residents and potential visitors.

Sending routine media releases and photos to outlets outside the event host area may get some pick-up, but for each mile away from that city, percentages of coverage spawned by uninspired publicity diminish. However, media use can be increased, often significantly, with generous applications of creativity and innovation.

One of the most effective techniques is called "borrowed localization." This technique directly involves media centers in an event taking place outside the area they normally serve. That is, it makes the event locally meaningful to news media in distant centers. This approach can best be illustrated by a strategy specifically designed for and tailored to a planned event, outlined on the following pages.

SOME BASIC PUBLICITY IDEAS

We are presenting below a few publicity ideas that have worked for a variety of special events. Even though they may not work as described here for your own happening, these ideas are presented to spur thinking and suggest creative approaches for publicity that can, in fact, work well for you.

Area Talent Search

You can generate publicity through individualized media releases to outlying areas, calling for performers to audition for your event. Additionally, those who are selected become the subjects of hometowners before and during the festival.

Sports Participants

The same approach applies to sports. ("Sports Enthusiasts Invited to Festival Tournaments.") Follow-up releases cover those who registered for golf, etc. Eventually, of course, winners are hometowned.

Visitors With Special Needs

Contact churches and humanitarian organizations throughout your market region, inviting them to sponsor bus trips to the event for such groups as the indigent, the elderly, and the disabled. News media often help with such efforts by promoting contributions through their airtime or in their pages. With the permission of the sponsoring groups, announcements in media at points of origin ahead of their visits and coverage during the festival would serve to credit host groups for their altruism.

Outside Purchases

Most events rightfully have a policy of buying locally whenever possible. However, rarely will all needs be met by outlets within the host city. When "interesting" purchases (2 lbs. of no. 10 nails is not interesting-, 200 tons of those nails is!) must be made away from home, put out the information to both your local media and *especially* media in the area of purchase.

Sponsors

News of a sponsor-event alliance is very frequently worthy of coverage by media, again both in home territory and around the headquarters market. Working closely with sponsors, check into possible coverage in trade publications and other media of specific interest to the sponsoring organization.

Visiting Media

Event publicity specialists should initiate their contacts with outlying media at least six months ahead of opening day. Personal visits are recommended over mailings. Media personnel should be invited to cover an event and plans should be outlined for providing them with well-trained media aides. At the event, the marketing unit should make every effort to put visiting media in contact with residents of their home areas. This effort can be facilitated through a Visitor Reception Desk in the main festival operations center. An idea seed can be planted during early contacts with outlying media by suggesting that they make advance arrangements for covering groups in their areas who will be attending the festival. This procedure can be easily accomplished throughout the event marketing area especially in small towns and rural locales.

Smaller media—community daily and weekly newspapers and limited-range radio stations—can play a major role in outlying publicity strategy. Not only are they more likely to use supplied hand-outs than their larger metro counterparts, but also their readership and listener numbers are often surprisingly impressive. Further, their message absorption levels are often percentage-wise as high or higher than those produced by big-city media. Material that is as camera-ready as possible and is prepared with the borrowed localization angle stands a better chance of being used.

Meaningful working arrangements with distant metro media almost always start with a personal, direct-contact visit. Rarely will big city media use canned material verbatim from any source. In-person conferences with carefully selected people on sports, feature, and other assignment desks should be arranged. At these conferences, present plenty of professionally prepared, locally angled material. This type of hand-out is the most likely to produce results.

In media programs for both the host area and outlying markets, effective publicists never forget coverage opportunities provided by high school and college newspapers, church bulletins, company newsletters, and other special-interest publications.

PUBLICITY WITHIN THE HOST CITY

Knowledgeable event promoters realize that most non-routine happenings during the preopening development period call for media involvement. Not just notification, *involvement!*

This means informing all news outlets of every board and committee meeting, giving them the gist of proposed business, and letting them choose whether to cover the gathering with their representatives or to take phoned or written accounts of it from the event public relations folks.

Involvement also means working with media in the preparation, production, and distribution of the festival calendar of events and any other wide-circulation material. Media people can also contribute additional talent as committee members or volunteers.

Media involvement can take the form of outright sponsorship of certain event segments. Some of the most workable sponsorship programs in special events are those centering around news outlets in the host cities. Television and radio stations often broadcast from their own on-site event locations, newspaper sponsors frequently provide informational and other services from booths or tents, and some media participate in traditional name-credit sponsorship roles.

Every news medium should be involved—all metro dailies, specialty publications, weekly newspapers, magazines, radio stations, and certainly television. Here is a partial list of topics potentially rich in media interest.

- Annual naming of administrative hierarchy— new chairpersons, committee heads, etc.

- Interviews with new festival leaders regarding their hopes, plans, etc.

- Annual announcement of the theme for the coming event

- Annual announcement of poster and any other artwork competitions, with follow-up when winners are chosen

- Annual volunteer appreciation and recognition dinner

- Announcements of sponsorships (Again, sponsorship is a very important need. Media in many host cities recognize that and thus are more lenient than usual about commercialism in their editorial material. They are generally pretty good about permitting reasonable company and product name mentions related to event sponsorships.)

- Announcements of major event elements, such as shows, headliners and other talent appearances, outstanding sport participants, additions to the line-up of offerings, etc.

- Significant changes in the event's physical layout, policies, shows, philosophy, timing, etc.

- Announcement of the detailed event program and timetable (possible newspaper insert or special section)

- Hints for event-goers what to wear; where to park; sun protection; special facilities for infants, the elderly, the disabled etc.

- Information about visiting dignitaries

- Post-event summary of operation, attendance, income, expenses, etc.

A member of the publicity unit within the marketing group should attend every committee meeting, unless advance notice is given that a meeting is going to be either too technical or only a working operation from which no news could possibly be gleaned. A surprising amount of newsworthy material can be generated in committee meetings. News summaries should be immediately forwarded to media not in attendance.

NATIONAL AND REGIONAL PUBLICITY

Even a first-time event can claim a portion of the national media spotlight. We suggest the following techniques in order to develop a national publicity program for your event.

Travel Editor Mailings

Artists' renderings of events that are "supposed to happen" are not generally highly favored for publication by travel editors. However, even with use probabilities somewhat low, a well-prepared package should be readied and distributed prior to the initial event, especially to travel editors throughout the designated marketing area. Such material, if not published, may spark column mentions or shorter stories. At any rate, these items begin what must become a constant effort to educate editors about and sell them on the quality of the event.

Because of the extraordinary competition for travel publication space among summer activities, it was suggested that material for summer events be distributed no later then April 1 of the year of the first festival for daily and weekly publications and by January 15 for major monthly publications. Few large monthly travel magazines publish unsolicited material, but such items can spawn interest in staff- or free-lance-written stories. And remember: most monthly magazines have deadlines as far as 120 days or more ahead of publication and may plan issues a full year in advance.

Quality photos are the crux of good travel material. The highest priority should be given to providing a selection of excellent artwork for every mailing.

Travel writers often complain about stories that are too lengthy. Therefore, festival copy should be limited to two full double-spaced pages. Included in each package should be a fact sheet from which travel writers can pick up additional information or develop their own copy.

800 Number

If it is affordable, install an 800 information line well ahead of the festival opening. Its number should be prominently displayed in all printed and publicity material.

Chase's Annual Events

Virtually every television and radio station, newspaper, magazine, most advertising groups, public relations agencies, libraries, and entertainment-related entities, and thousands of individuals throughout the nation purchase *Chase's Annual Events*. This publication is the best and most complete compendium of holidays, tournaments, national and ethnic days, seasons, festivals, fairs, anniversaries, birthdays, special events, and traditional observances. To be listed in *Chase's* requires only the submission of the coming event in the prescribed format on a form that can be obtained from:

Chase's Calendar of Events
Contemporary Books, Inc.
2 Prudential Plaza, Suite 1200
Chicago, IL 60601
Phone: (847) 679-5500
Fax: (847) 679-2494

The completed form must be returned to Chase's by early May of the year prior to the year of the happening. Item inclusion in this publication can magnetize a surprising amount of national publicity, especially if an event is truly unusual, large or new. There is no cost for this listing, and the coming year's edition may be purchased in December prior to that year.

IEG Sponsorship Report

The bible of the event marketing industry is the *IEG Sponsorship Report* newsletter. Sponsorship and basic information on events should be supplied when appropriate to this important, twice monthly publication. The address:

Lesa Ukman, Executive Editor
IEG Sponsorship Report
IEG, Inc.
640 North LaSalle, Suite 600
Chicago, IL 60610-3777
Phone: (312) 944-1727
Fax: (312) 944-1897

Publishers of the *IEG Sponsorship Report* also host the International Events Group (IEG) Sponsorship Conference in March of each year in Chicago. Every event can benefit from representation at these meetings.

Familiarization Visits

Another recommendation in the Boise study was to make every effort to host familiarization visits to the festival by travel editors and writers as well as travel agents.

Most media policies prohibit travel-desk personnel from accepting trips paid for by host organizations, but good selling jobs can entice them to set aside some of their budget for coverage of worthy events.

ADVERTISING

As previously stated, limited budgets mean limited advertising, generally.

However, a line item showing a minimum sum must be included in budgets of all but the smallest events. This amount will pay for such items as a minimum number of audition calls in selected publications, promotions in printed programs of surrounding events, and ad hoc miscellaneous opportunities.

For non-profit events, printed advertisements and aired commercials will often be carried free of charge by the media as public service announcements (PSAs). In other instances, such material is paid for through sponsor dollars or provided as a direct in-kind sponsorship of the event.

Bill Stuffers

Every month, millions of supplied messages are included in bills sent out by telephone, utility, and other billing companies. Often, this service can be pinpointed for recipients within given area codes. It is one of the most efficient and cost-effective direct mail services available, and every event should investigate bill-stuffer opportunities existing in its marketing areas.

Inserts should be expertly produced sales pieces, listing as many event assets as possible and spelling out solutions to such needs as advance lodging arrangements. The insert might also include a simple city map, contact addresses and phone numbers, etc.

Because printing large quantities of stuffers of reasonable quality can be expensive, some events have lined up commercial sponsors to pick up the tab in exchange for credit on the mailing piece, bannering, and signage throughout the event.

Bus and Taxi Cards

Often, as good corporate citizens and as their special contribution to a city event, transportation companies will make exterior display-card space available at discounted rates or even without charge to local non-profit happenings.

On-Premise Promotions

Your marketing plan section should emphasize the need to line up as many local public operations and facilities as possible to carry promotional posters and banners as early as two months before the opening day of the festival. These operations and facilities include both commercial and noncommercial establishments. Contact calls should include suggestions for self-designed and executed promotions by these establishments. Examples of such promotions include the following:

- Special product packaging that promotes the event
- Themed street windows and in-store displays (special plaques or trophies could be presented for outstanding examples)
- Lobby displays in banks, hotels, office buildings, colleges, airports, etc. (again, plaques or trophies to winners)

On-Pack/In-Pack Contests and Offers

Your event representatives should visit consumer product companies asking that on-pack/in-pack contests and offers become a part of event promotions (promotional incentives that are included as part of a product's packaging, either on-pack or in-pack depending on the product; e.g., contest entry forms). A number of types of offers exist, each thoroughly familiar to promotions managers, that provide to people in outlying areas such rewards as all-expenses-paid visits to the event. Lesser prizes, available to local residents as well as those in more distant areas, include festival souvenirs, merchandise, food and beverage coupons, etc.

Invitational Post Cards

Consider the production of attractive post cards featuring enticing festival artwork (after the first festival, photos can be used). These postcards can be distributed on a limited basis without charge beginning six months ahead of the opening day.

Host city residents can be encouraged to pick up cards for mailing to family and friends outside their metro area, calling attention to the coming event and hopefully inviting them to be their guests while attending the big happening.

This promotion is especially appealing to sponsors because their names, logos, short messages, etc., can be incorporated into the card design, thus spreading their participation—and credit—far and wide.

Souvenir Programs and Brochures

The schedule of events, especially when published as an attractive sell-oriented guidebook, is one of the most important aspects of event promotion and enjoyment, even for smaller happenings.

This publication must spell out clearly the times and locations of all events, provide easily fol-

lowed maps, and include necessary information for the safety and comfort of guests, first aid station locations, parking restrictions, lost children/parent reunion points, etc.

Another important publication is a general wrap-up brochure that should serve as both the spine for the sponsorship solicitation efforts and the overall general sales piece for the event. This wrap-up brochure should be included in media kits and should be available for mailing in response to inquiries from outlying areas.

Advertising space in both publications should offset most or all production costs. Whenever possible, these publications should be created by top-line graphic artists and produced by the highest quality print shops. Because these publications represent the event, contribute significantly to the enjoyment of the event, and serve as primary sales pieces for sponsors and advertisers, their importance warrants efforts to assure the highest quality.

■ SECTION 2 ■

WIN-WIN SPONSORSHIP

Chapter Seven

FIRST THINGS FIRST: PREPARING FOR SPONSORSHIP

Sponsorship is one of those unusual phenomena that just seemed to appear in our lives one day. No one really noticed; it just appeared. And, like other similar phenomena of our time (the fax machine, for instance), no one can imagine what we ever did without it.

Just about every part of our lives is touched by sponsorship: sports events; performance venues; movie premiers; concerts; art exhibits; videos; fairs and festivals; car, boat, plane, and home shows; individual athletes; trade shows; parades; special anniversaries; city celebrations; fireworks; museums; amusement parks; and cause-related fund raisers. The list goes on and on.

Sponsorship—the use of financial or in-kind support of an on-business activity by a commercial organization to achieve specified business goals—has become the foundation of today's event industry. Many events would not exist without sponsorship support. For many others, it spells the difference between quality, size, outreach and success. In a dramatic change of position, even the United States Armed Services now approves the solicitation of corporate sponsorship to support the increase of quality events and recreational programs for armed service personnel and their families around the world.

However, sponsorship is not without its critics. Over-commercialism, control of athletes or sporting events (especially with the expansion of sponsorship into college sports), and the funneling of corporate dollars from more critical concerns (e.g. hunger, homelessness, and health issues) are just some of the criticisms aimed at corporate sponsors. To date, however, the event industry has no established an accepted governing organization to set ethical standards and much needed formal training programs.

We proceed here with the assumption that readers of this book are in favor of sponsorship and are interested in how to expand their expertise and understanding in the areas of sponsorship solicitation and consideration. We discuss the future and the needs of the industry in Chapter Twelve.

OBJECTIVE EVALUATION

Before hitting the streets to begin selling an event to potential sponsors, the first thing one must do is take a long, hard, objective look at the event itself. This isn't always easy to do. You must be objective. Admittedly mixing metaphors, like your child, you can love your event, but still recognize its faults; like selling a car, you must fix a few nicks and dings before you put it on the market.

Many people find they cannot muster this kind of objectivity and find it valuable to bring in an outside consultant to do an effective analysis. Whether you do it yourself or employ a consultant, the question you must answer is the same: "What can you do to make the event better?"

"Afflict the comfortable." —Carl Ally

Is the event old and tired or old and fresh? As we have emphasized before, because an event has been going on for years in the same way, or was

done that way in another location does not necessarily mean it is being done in the best possible way. Don't fall in love with one idea. New or old, look at your event and ask what you can do to offer sponsors and patrons something of value or greater value in a new way.

MAKE STRENGTHS STRONGER AND REPLACE WEAKNESSES

Look at the strengths of the event and, rather than be satisfied, make them stronger. Survey the audience or look to ticket sales and other predictors of satisfaction. Once strengths have been identified build on them. Consider adding more of the cements that are popular. Findings may warrant expanding (or reducing) the length of run. Whatever increases your audience attendance and satisfaction makes the event more valuable to potential sponsors. Similarly, discard or replace weaknesses once they have become apparent.

Analyze the competition and similar events in other locations. Note what they are doing that might add to your event. Change for the sake of change is not good, but change to keep an event fresh and growing is essential.

Many events are hurt by politics that dictate event elements and prohibit necessary change and growth. While it may be impossible to eliminate this problem totally, the use of an outside consultant can sometimes help enormously. An outside opinion can often carry weight not afforded to those staff members who work with an event every day. Unfortunately, many organizations do not recognize and fully use the talent and expertise that they have at their fingertips.

BE CREATIVE

There is a definite line that separates trend setters and trend followers, and that line is creativity. A creative person looks at the same thing as everyone else and thinks something different. This ability is especially valuable in the special events industry. Use creativity to provide something unique. As discussed in Chapter Four, most events tend to be annual "reproductions" rather than annual productions. A truly unique event will draw sponsors out of the woodwork.

In the July 10, 1989, issue of *Special Events Report* (now the *IEG Sponsorship Report*), it is noted that the "copycat syndrome" is a primary reason that sponsors do not stick with what they start sponsoring. Companies hate "me, too" events. Companies sponsor events to stand out from their competitors, not to emulate them.

If your creative muscle needs exercising, we recommend reading *A Whack on the Side of the Head* and *A Kick in the Seat of the Pants*, by Roger von Oech, Ph.D., Founder and President of Creative Think. Both books should be available at local bookstores and should become an indispensable part of any library.

Expand the creative horizon. Invite outside sources in for brainstorming sessions. Representatives from sponsor, patron, and media groups (supporters and critics) may offer many worthwhile suggestions; and don't ignore the ideas and talents of in-house staff. There is no shortage of ideas, but these ideas need to be used in order to make a difference.

In many cases, something as simple as a new paint job, different graphics, improved maintenance, or better costumes can make a world of difference in an event. The Disney organization has perfected this skill. Go to a Disney theme park and look around. There is virtually no litter or areas in disrepair because Disney realizes the importance of these impressions and has created systems to maintain a "magical" place.

In his book, *Thriving on Chaos,* Tom Peters comments that what they need to teach in business school is "Toilets 101." He goes on to explain that if a client goes into a Fortune 500 company and finds their restrooms are a mess, it will affect that client's perception of the entire company. The same rule applies to events.

And, finally, ask "What if?" questions about the event. For example, what if Walt Disney ran this event? How would the event be run?

DEFINING SPONSOR OPPORTUNITIES

Now that the event has been evaluated, and its position strengthened, it is time to define just what there is to offer to potential sponsors. The event marketers must be confident of what they are selling.

Does the event provide media opportunities? Opportunities for brand promotions? Can it reach a wide cross-section of the community? Walk through the event and decide. The determination of what there is to offer narrows the focus of who should be approached regarding sponsorship.

A good starting point is to review the seven basic sponsor objectives in Chapter One and list the areas where your event provides opportunities to meet those objectives for a sponsor. If one area is obviously lacking in opportunities, fix it. For example, for sponsors wanting to meet Objective 3— positive publicity—it is necessary to list every publicity opportunity and other means of attracting positive attention that your event offers. Your list may look something like this:

- Media coverage (include advertising, press releases, media co-sponsor commitments, etc.)
- Banners (list all locations, sizes, etc.)
- Posters
- Brochure/Program inclusions
- Verbal credit
- Tickets, etc.

These opportunities may also be a part of your list for Objective 1—image building and enhancement, and Objective 5—good corporate citizen.

In most cases you will be selling one or both of two broad goal categories to potential sponsors: awareness/image, and trial/sampling opportunities. Note: if offering trial-sampling opportunities, are audiences controlled (tickets required, set entrances/exits to venue) or uncontrolled (spread out, no set entrances/exits)? This will be important to potential sponsors.

Next, determine what the impact area is. This refers to the media reach from which the event draws.

Is the event:
International (e.g., the Olympics)
National (e.g., the Pasadena Tournament of Roses Parade)
Regional (e.g., the Taste of Chicago Festival) or
Local (e.g., Tucson Meet Yourself)?

Be honest when determining the impact area. One lone mention in a *USA Today* calendar does not make an event national, and sponsors know that. Besides, there is a new trend in sponsorship today to market more on a regional or targeted local level, eliminating the pressure to be nationally oriented and increasing the value of smaller, quality events.

FIND A NICHE AND BE THE BEST

After all of the evaluating and fine tuning, you should have found your niche. No event or product can be all things to all people, and it shouldn't try to be. It is better to offer less with more quality.

This means that a given event can't be sold to everybody. For example, because of the type of image "Up With People," the international performing group, has chosen as their niche, they must be cautious when considering sponsors from the alcohol, religion, tobacco, and political areas. However, because they offer the best in their niche of entertainment, there is no shortage of sponsors from other categories.

Don't approach sponsorship strictly from a monetary basis. If a sponsorship combination isn't right, it will cause more problems than opportunities and won't work for anyone involved.

CHAPTER EIGHT

RIFLE-SHOT RESEARCH

THE PURPOSE OF RESEARCH AND TARGETING

Researching and targeting sponsors is probably the most overlooked and undervalued step in the sponsorship solicitation process. While it requires some up-front time, the rewards down the road include higher quality sponsorships and fewer rejections. Research and targeting mean carefully sighted, predetermined rifle shots as opposed to the scattergun approach ("Just mail out as many sponsorship proposals and computerized cover letters as you can, and you're bound to get some sponsors.")

Guilt is one of the reasons those in the events industry don't do more research and targeting. If they are not on the telephone making a call (worthless or not), they feel like they aren't doing their jobs. Or, if their boss walks in and they are reading a magazine article or newspaper story about a potential sponsor, it looks like they aren't working. Or, the worst scenario of all, they don't know how or where to research.

Chances are the boss appreciates the value of research and targeting, so guilt is unnecessary. The "how" and "where" are very necessary, however, so we address them here. The purpose of research is to assimilate useful information, regarding the potential sponsor(s) or sponsor category, that can then be incorporated into a targeted sales strategy that best meets the sponsors needs. To do that, one must first understand those needs.

For instance, don't ask Mack Truck to sponsor the Royal Canadian Ballet. It just doesn't fit. A good fit, on the other hand, is Pepto-Bismol and the World Championship Chili Cook-off. The closer the event skews to the sponsor's positioning, the easier the sale.

TYPES OF SPONSORS

There are several different forms of sponsorship to be aware of before beginning the search. Sponsors may fall into more than one category, and these multiple categories provide opportunities for a variety of sponsors to participate in the event at varying levels of financial commitment:

Exclusive or Title Sponsor

Title sponsors pay a premium fee to have their name as part of the event itself (e.g., the Tostitos Fiesta Bowl). Exclusive sponsors pay extra to close out potential sponsorships by competitive or similar sponsors/products (e.g., the "Official Beer of the NFL"). Title sponsors are usually exclusive.

Presenting Sponsor

Sponsors at this level are usually the major sponsor of a predetermined portion of the entire event (e.g., Kodak presents the halftime spectacular of the Tostitos Fiesta Bowl).

Co-sponsor

Co-sponsors, as implied, share event sponsorship with one or more other sponsors. There can be co-sponsors at all levels, but title sponsorship is usually exclusive.

Media Sponsor

Media sponsors usually provide a predetermined amount of advertising support for the event. They may also provide some cash support and publicity. Note: selection of a media sponsor may negate support from other similar media. Be sure the advertising provided is worth that. A new event, especially, should be careful about locking into only one media, as support will be needed from all sources.

In-Kind Sponsor

Sponsorship on this level is provided through the donation of products or services. While cash does not trade hands, in-kind support helps to lower event expenses.

CREATE A PROSPECT LIST

Start by compiling a list of categories and companies who would most likely be interested in sponsoring your event. "Most likely" can be established by responding "yes" to all or most of the following questions about each candidate/ category:

1. Does the prospective sponsor sell or operate in the event's host community?

2. Does the prospective sponsor's history include past or present sponsorship? If so, what kind?

3. Does the prospective sponsor advertise in the host community?

4. Does the prospective sponsor maintain a high profile in the host community?

5. Is the prospective sponsor's name mentioned with some frequency in the news media? (Is it mentioned for positive or negative reasons?)

6. Does the prospective sponsor provide a commercial function that is customer- or client-driven?

7. Is the prospective sponsor noted for the support of at least some altruistic or community betterment efforts?

Don't stop with the initial list. Explore new areas. Network with other people. Get introductions. Sometimes the obvious escapes those closest to it. Sources to network through may include:

*   Past and current sponsors
*   Associates and peers
*   Group ownership counterparts
*   Professional association members

From the "most likely" list, develop an accurate prospect or candidate list. Call and check names and titles of those who handle sponsorship for each company. Names and positions change frequency—proposals have been sent to dead people! Better to check now than be embarrassed later.

WALK IN THE SPONSOR'S SHOES

Before approaching a potential sponsor, use research to learn about their business. Put yourself in their shoes. Sponsors are hit with thousands of messages daily. General Mills receives up to 4,000 sponsorship requests annually; Coca-Cola and Anheuser-Busch receive ten times that many. Some airlines receive as many as 100 requests daily for support. All these figures mean that one must do everything possible to beat the odds, target their approach, and keep from getting lost in the clutter.

Read trade journals, and ask for copies of annual reports. Look for trends, problems, and opportunities in the sponsors' industry. Learn their terminology so that you can communicate with them better.

Care about what they do. Find out who buys or uses their product or service. Consider whether the event reaches those people most important to that potential sponsor. Learn how they market their product or service and what their advertising strategy is. Be able to say, "I understand what you are trying to do. Now let me explain how we can help you do chat."

If possible, ask current or potential sponsors if you might spend some time with them to get a better handle on their problems or needs. Think about how you can help fulfill their corporate goals in terms of seven basic objectives discussed in Chapter One (repeated here for quick reference).

1.   Image Enhancement
2.   Drive Sales
3.   Positive Publicity
4.   Differentiate Product from Competitors
5.   Good Corporate Citizen
6.   Community Economic Development
7.   Customer / VIP Relations

Look at what they currently do and where they want to go, and think of how to translate that into what there is to sell. Consider their perspective and ask, "How will this benefit me?"

ANOTHER SHOT TO BE CREATIVE

We've discussed the importance of evaluating the event and making it unique. It is also important to use creative abilities and brainstorming sessions to benefit a potential sponsor.

Based upon research, ask yourself, "What does this company need?" Now, what program or benefits can be created to meet their needs by way of the event? A targeted and personalized approach to any potential sponsor indicates that homework has been done. This increases the likelihood of being given serious consideration. For example, because of the "Exxon Valdez" oil spill, Exxon desperately needed to repair and enhance their image nationally and, particularly, in Alaska. How could your event help them?

RESEARCH—THE NEXT GENERATION (WHERE MANY PEOPLE HAVE NEVER GONE BEFORE)

Now that it's clear how important and valuable research can be, here are additional areas to examine as well:

The sales targets

Are your prospective sponsors experienced or inexperienced when it comes to event marketing? This will affect your approach. Does the person you're approaching have the authority to make decisions? To answer this question, simply ask when making the appointment. Don't let a subordinate present your plan to a superior if possible. You are your own best salesperson.

The event competition

Competitors are a tremendous source of information. Ask for proposals, materials, and fee structures. Know and be a slave to the competition. Take their best ideas and make them better. If there is no direct competition, research similar events in other cities. We emphasize, however: *Improve on ideas, don't just steal them.*

The media

In each market, learn the number one television and radio station; the daily newspaper with the largest circulation; talk shows and program formats; and the weekly newspapers, magazines, and specialty publications available. Good media research goes a long way in creating a successful event.

RESEARCH SOURCES

We have provided in the pages that follow a "Corporate Sponsorship Research Guide" to help you begin the research process. This guide is taken in part from bibliographies by the staff and students of the University of Arizona, Tucson. The authors are deeply indebted to Susan Hurt of the University of Arizona for her assistance in our research for this book, and to Kaye Campbell of the Boise River Festival for its updating.

CORPORATE SPONSORSHIP RESEARCH GUIDE

In the quickly growing special events industry, research has become an essential ingredient in successfully positioning and selling corporate sponsorships. From a broad focus on targeted industries/markets to a more narrow look at individual companies, events, and the people who make the decisions regarding sponsorship dollars, good research can make the difference between those all important yes and no answers.

Research sources also offer us the ability to collect information about our competition and those crucial media sources that can help make or break an event.

This source list is meant to be a guide to that information that can aid us in better targeting our approaches. It is not meant to be an end-all, be-all, source, but rather a beginning for our creative styles and ideas to take form. There are many other sources of information besides those listed here, depending on the information you are searching for. You will begin to develop your own favorite sources as you go.

Most of the sources on this list are available in the reference section at your local library, although it should be noted that all libraries do not have the same reference sources. If yours does not have a particular source, ask your librarian for help. He or she can direct you to other sources or help you find the one you need. University or college libraries are usually the best sources of reference information. If you desire, many of these sources may be purchased for your office or home use.

The "Other Resources" section of this list is a culmination of directories and publications, including ongoing newsletters, that are recognized sources of information in the special events industry today. Most of these will not be available in your library, but addresses and phone numbers are provided so that you may order them directly from the publisher. There will most likely be a cost or subscription fee involved for these.

Of course in today's high-tech information society, computers provide one of the most readily accessible stores of information through sources such as CD-Rom directories, world-wide web pages, and on-line services. Modems even make it possible to view these sources from the comfort of your own home. If you do not have access to a personal computer, check with your local library. Most have now converted to some sort of on-line system.

Good luck and happy researching!

INDUSTRY INFORMATION

Most of the sources listed in this section can be found in your library reference section. To update the information available in books, look for current articles in newspapers and periodicals on the industry. To do this, check the periodical indexes listed in this guide. The best ones for industry information are INFOTRAC and PREDICASTS F & S INDEX.

• **Standard & Poor's Industry Surveys (quarterly)**

This is like an encyclopedia on American industries. There are 69 industries covered, and for each industry there is information about the trends, problems, and future outlook. Leading companies in each industry are identified and compared. In the front of each volume is a subject or product index and a company name index.

• **U.S. Industrial Outlook (annual)**

Published by the Commerce Department, this annual profiles approximately 200 industries. The outlook, or future trend for each, is given for five years. This source does not identify the leading companies.

• **Forbes Magazine "Annual Report on American Industry" (annual)**

This article appears in the January issue of *Forbes* magazine every year. It gives an overview of each industry and a ranking of the leading companies in each industry.

• **Value Line Investment Survey (weekly)**

This is an investment service advising buyers on stock selections. It is useful for both company and industry information. Part One is "Summary & Index". Part Two is a weekly "Selections & Opinions", which has Value Line's views on business and economics outlook. Part Three, "Rating & Reports", is the most important section. It is divided by industry. For each industry, there is a one- to two-page overview followed by a company-by-company profile of the most important public corporations in the industry.

• **Monthly Catalog of United States Government Publications (monthly)**

Federal documents are generally *not* listed in a library's card catalog. To locate government publications on industries, you need to use the Monthly Catalog, which is the most comprehensive index of government documents.

GUIDES TO BUSINESS & INDUSTRY LITERATURE

• **Business Information Sources**

This is an excellent guide to business information sources on almost any topic. Be certain to use the detailed index in the back.

• **Encyclopedia of Business Information Sources**

This lists the basic encyclopedias, handbooks, bibliographies, directories, periodicals, statistical sources, and general works on almost any product or industry, as well as the trade associations and professional societies.

• **Directory of Industry Data Sources, The United States of America & Canada**

Arranged by industry, this is a bibliography of marketing and financial sources.

ASSOCIATIONS

• **Encyclopedia of Associations (annual)**

A guide to national and international organizations—trades, business, commercial, legal, governmental, educational, etc.

• **National Trade & Professional Associations of the United States**

Identifies U.S. trade associations and describes their services and publications.

COMPANY INFORMATION

The sources listed in this part are divided into four sections:
1. Directories
2. Public Corporations
3. Private Companies, Franchises, and Small Firms
4. Company Rankings

Directories provide very brief information such as address, telephone number(s) , names of key personnel, and line of business. They are usually arranged alphabetically by company names and often have geographical sections (so you can locate companies in a certain city) and industry sections (so you can identify companies by industry or product).

Included in Section I are directories of subsidiaries and affiliates. These titles provide the "family trees" of companies so you can see the relationship of parents, subsidiaries and divisions. If a company is owned by another company and you need to find detailed financial information on the subsidiary, you will need to research the parent company and glean from these reports the information on the subsidiary. If there have been periodical articles on the subsidiary, you can locate these in the periodical indexes listed by subsidiary name.

For most purposes, you will need more information on companies than is provided in the company directories. The sources listed in Section 2 of this part provide detailed financial information and short histories or background information on private companies.

A search for financial information on a company can be very simple or very complicated depending on the type of company. If the company's stock is traded on the New York Stock Exchange (NYSE), or the American Stock Exchange (ASE), or Over-The-Counter (OTC), you will be able to find a wealth of descriptive and financial information. Other corporations, private companies, franchises, and local businesses are much more difficult to research because most of these firms are not required to disclose their financial situation. For these firms, you will use different sources than you use for the public corporations.

Section 4 includes books that rank companies. These are very useful when you are trying to identify the largest companies in the U.S. or the largest companies in an industry.

DIRECTORIES

U.S.

•   Hoover's Handbook of American Business (annual)

Profiles 500 of the largest and most influential companies in America. Contains the following four components:

- review of basic business concepts and profile contents
- lists of the largest companies in the book and the largest companies in various industries
- 500 major profiles, arranged alphabetically
- three indexes containing 1) companies organized by industry groupings, 2) companies organized by headquarters location, and 3) names of all brands, companies and people mentioned in the profiles.

•   Hoover's Handbook of Emerging Companies (annual)

Profiles 125 + of America's most exciting growth companies (some private), chosen for their demonstrated growth and potential for further gains. Company selections are based on the following criteria:

- must be U.S. based
- must have revenues between $30 million and $1 billion
- must have had sales growth of at least 20% per year annually or sales and net income growth of at least 15% each annually during the past five years.

•   Million Dollar Directory (annual)

Published in four separate volumes, this is a directory of over 160,000 U.S. businesses with a net worth of over $500,000. It is comprised of three volumes arranged alphabetically according to company name. The fourth volume is a SERIES CROSS-REFERENCE VOLUME. Here you can find a geographical approach or product (SIC) approach to the companies in the first three volumes.

• **DUN'S Account Identification Service (annual)**

This microfiche collection provides the address of virtually every business in the U.S.; nearly five million businesses are included.

Each listing includes name, DUN's number, and street address, and a headquarters or branch designation. Fuller information on companies with 10 or more employees is available through the on-line database DUN'S MARKET IDENTIFIERS 10 +.

• **Standard and Poor's Register of Corporations, Directors and Executives (annual)**

This three-volume annual includes directory information on 40,000 corporations. Volume I is arranged alphabetically by company names and includes address, telephone, names and titles of directors and officials, stock exchange information, description of primary business, SIC numbers, annual sales, and number of employees. Volume 11 provides biographical information on directors and executives. Volume III lists companies by SIC numbers (industrial classification) and by state and city. Volume III also includes an index of subsidiaries and divisions and an obituary section.

• **Standard Directory of Advertisers (annual)**

This directory lists over 17,000 companies that advertise nationally or regionally. It includes many companies difficult to locate in other directories. Companies are listed by product classification. Listings include name, address, phone, type of business, key management personnel, advertising agency, amount spent on advertising, and media used. There is an alphabetical company name index and a trade name list.

• **Standard Directory of Advertising Agencies (tri-annual)**

This publication lists approximately 4,400 agencies in the U.S. and overseas. Indexed by location and by markets served, it is published three times a year.

• **Rand McNally International Bankers Directory (annual)**

This directory lists U.S. and international banks.

• **Thomas Register of American Manufacturers (annual)**

This is a directory of manufacturing businesses in the U.S. The major volumes are arranged by product and list the companies that manufacture that product. The "Company Profile" volumes list all companies alphabetically and give address, telephone product and a size rating by tangible assets. A brand name index is included in the Company Profile volumes. Accompanying the register are catalogs from selected companies.

DIVISIONS AND SUBSIDIARIES

• **America's Corporate Families: The Billion Dollar Directory (annual)**

The purpose of this book is to show the corporate family structure of U.S. corporations. Section I lists the top 500 parent companies. The information on each company is similar to the information in the *Million Dollar Directory* and is followed by a list of all divisions and subsidiaries. Section 11, the geographical section, lists the parents and subsidiaries by state and city. Section III classifies each business by SIC numbers.

• **Directory of Corporate Affiliations (annual)**

Similar to *America's Corporate Families*, this directory lists NYSE and ASE companies, the Fortune 1000, and many privately owned and OTC companies. Section I lists all divisions, subsidiaries and affiliates and gives the page number in Section 11 where the parent companies and their "family trees" are listed. Part II also contains directory information on each parent, subsidiary, division and affiliate.

- ### Who Owns Whom — North American Edition (annual)

This directory shows the corporate family structure of U.S. companies with non-U.S. subsidiaries or associates and of Canadian companies with subsidiaries or associates in the U.S. Part I lists U.S. parents and their corporate addresses; beneath each parent is a list of its subsidiaries and associates and their country location. Part II includes the same information for Canadian parents. Part III is an index to subsidiary and associate names and gives their parent company's name.

- ### PTS Company Directory (annual)

This directory lists more than 125,000 company names. Includes preferred spelling, divisions, subsidiaries, and country in which each company is headquartered.

INTERNATIONAL

- ### Principal International Businesses (annual)

This is a directory of over 50,000 leading businesses worldwide. The main section is arranged by country and includes the line of business, sales volume, number of employees, chief executive's name and title, address, and name of the parent company. In Part II, all businesses are arranged by product classification. Part III is an alphabetical list of all companies included, which is particularly valuable if you do not know what country the company is located in.

- ### Bottin International (annual)

Similar in purpose to *Principal International Businesses,* this is a directory of international companies. The main section is arranged by country; Volume I includes all countries except European countries; Volume II covers all European countries. Within each country, businesses are listed by product. In addition to company information, this work includes basic information on countries useful to businessmen, such as a listing of banks, advertising agencies, and hotels.

- ### Ward's Business Directory of Major International Companies (annual)

Over 15,000 corporate listings in three sections—geographic, Standard Industrial Classifications, and alphabetic. Includes company rankings by sales and number of employees.

PUBLIC CORPORATIONS

Financial and background information on publicly owned companies is readily available because these companies must file a 1O-K report disclosing their financial situation to the Securities and Exchange Commission and send an annual report to their stockholders. Moody's and Standard and Poor's both obtain these reports and condense the facts in their publications. These two services are the first place to look for detailed information on a public company. If more information is needed, you can use the 1O-K Report and Annual Reports; they are usually available on microfiche.

Although you should be able to find detailed descriptive and financial information on public companies, you may want to search for newspaper and periodical articles on these companies also. Using indexes is the most efficient way to find articles. The best indexes to use are *INFOTRAC, Predicasts F&S Index United States,* and the *Wall Street Journal Index.*

- ### Moody's Manuals (annual plus updates)

Moody's has taken the information available on corporations traded on the NYSE, ASE, regional exchanges, and OTC companies and condensed it to one to five pages for each company. To facilitate research of several similar corporations, Moody's has divided the companies by type of business into the following separate volumes:

Bank and Finance Manual
Industrial Manual
Municipal and Government Manual
OTC Industrial Manual
Public Utility Manual
Transportation Manual
International Manual

Each manual has a detailed company name index including cross references to subsidiaries and name changes in the front of each volume. If you are unsure of which manual to consult, check *Moody's Complete Corporate Index*. It will refer you to the correct manual. For each company, there is a brief history; a list of subsidiaries, principal plants and properties, business and products, officers and directors; income statements; balance sheets; and financial rations. In the middle of each volume are blue pages that contain a wealth of useful information relevant to that type of business.

• Standard Corporation Records (annual plus updates)

This seven-volume financial service is comparable to *Moody's Manuals*. In order to use this service, first select the volume which, according to the letters on the spine, includes the company name. Then, check the yellow alphabetical index in the front of that volume. Here you will find page numbers for the main profile and updates on that company. For weekly updates, check the *Daily News* volume.

• Walker's Manual of Western Corporations (annual)

This publication has detailed financial information on publicly owned financial institutions/corporations headquartered in the western states.

• Company Filings

University or college libraries usually receive corporate filings from all companies on the NYSE, ASE, OTC and other exchanges. The two most common filings are the Annual Report to the Shareholders (ARS) and the 1O-K. Ask your librarian to help you find these.

• Annual Report to Shareholders

The Annual Report to Shareholders is the principal document used by *most* companies to disclose corporate information to shareholders and the public. The ARS is not a required filing and, therefore, great discretion is left to the company as to what information will be included. It is usually a state-of-the-company report including an opening letter

from the Chief Executive Officer, financial data, results of continuing operations, market segment information, new product plans, subsidiary activities, and research and development activities.

• 1O-K

The 1O-K is the annual report most reporting companies file with the Securities and Exchange Commission (SEC). It provides a comprehensive overview of the company. The key items it contains are a description of the business and of properties; legal proceedings; matters submitted to a vote of shareholders; management's discussion and analysis of financial conditions; financial data and statements; and list of directors and executive officers (including executive compensation).

• Proxy Statements

Proxy statements provide a good source for detailed information on corporate officers, usually including pictures, a brief biography and executive compensation.

PRIVATE COMPANIES, FRANCHISES AND SMALL FIRMS

Information on small or privately owned companies is very difficult and sometimes impossible to find. These companies do not have to release financial information unless they choose to do so. You will not be able to find information similar to the Moody's reports on private companies. This is true even if the private company's net worth is enormous.

One possible way to locate information on small firms and privately held companies is to look for newspaper and periodical articles about the company. The best indexes to use are Predicasts F & S Index United States, *Wall Street Journal Index*, INFOTRAC, and the *Business Periodicals Index*.

Another possible search strategy is to locate a special directory. The *Directory of Directories* is an annotated guide to all kinds of published directories. There is a subject index in the back. Each entry describes the publication and provides ordering information. A library may own many, but not all, of the directories listed.

- ### Ward's Directory of 49, 000 Private U.S. Companies

Lists private companies with $1-10 million in sales. Indexed listings are alphabetical, geographical, and by industry.

COMPANY RANKINGS

- ### Ward's Directory of 51,000 Largest U.S. Corporations

This is the most comprehensive ranking directory. It includes 8,000 public companies and 43,000 private companies. The following sections are included:

- 1,000 most profitable U.S. corporations
- 1,000 fastest growing U.S. corporations
- 1,000 largest publicly held corporations
- 1,000 largest privately held corporations
- 1,000 largest U.S. employers
- Total sales, employees, and number of companies in each SIC
- Total sales, employees, and number of companies in each state

- ### Dun's Business Rankings (annual)

This publication ranks over 7,500 U.S. public and private companies by annual sales and number of employees. Ranking by sales and number of employees is given for each state and for each industry group.

- ### Directory of U.S. Corporations (annual)

Commonly known as the Fortune Double 500, this annual ranks the 500 largest industrial companies and the 100 largest banks in the world; gives headquarter location, industry, sales assets, net income, stock holders' equity, and number of employees.

- ### Fortune World Business Directory (annual)

This directory features the 500 largest industrial companies and the 100 largest banks in the world; gives headquarter location, industry, sales assets, net income, stockholders' equity, and number of employees.

PERIODICALS, NEWSPAPERS, AND INDEXES

PERIODICALS AND NEWSPAPERS

In the field of business, currency is of vital importance. Investors and businessmen need to know what the financial situation is today and what the forecast is for next week and next year. Because of this, newspapers and periodicals are more important in business research than books. The lag time between when an author finishes writing a book and its publication is often over a year. Periodical articles are far more current.

Many business journals have special issues that are extremely valuable. Two of the more famous special issues are "The Fortune 500" and "Forbes Annual Report on American Industry". To locate other special issues of business journals use the *Guide to Industry Special Issues* or the *Special Issues Index: Specialized Contents of Business, Industrial, and Consumer Journals.*

At most libraries the current issues of popular periodicals are kept on hand. Back issues of periodicals are either bound and sent to their appropriate call number in the book stacks or purchased on microfilm.

Although all periodicals and newspapers received at the library are usually listed in the card catalog or computer reference system, it is best to check with a librarian.

INDICES

The most efficient way to locate periodical and newspaper articles is to use indexes. The following is a list of indexes to business materials.

•   Business Periodicals Index (monthly)

This is a subject index to articles in the major English language business magazines. It is the best known business index and is produced by the company that publishes *Reader's Guide*. All companies, products, industries, and business topics are listed in one alphabetical list. Broad topics are subdivided into subheadings.

•   InfoTrac (monthly)

Available via computer, InfoTrac indexes approximately 1,000 business, technical, and general magazines. Search by company name or topic.

•   Predicasts F & S Index — United States (weekly)

This index is an excellent source for industry, product and company information. It indexes over 750 financial and business publications, including many trade journals. Key articles are identified by a black dot before the name of the periodical. It is divided into two sections: Section I (colored pages) is arranged numerically by SIC number. An alphabetical index to SIC numbers is provided at the beginning of Section I. Section II (white pages) is arranged alphabetically by company name.

•   Predicasts F & S Index — Europe

This publication covers the European community, Scandinavia and eastern European countries. Includes company operations in Europe. In three sections: industries and products, countries and regions, and companies.

•   Predicasts F & S Index — International

Covers Canada, Latin American, Africa, the Mid-East, Asia, and Oceania. In three sections: industries and products, countries and regions, and companies.

•   Wall Street Journal Index (monthly)

Although the *Wall Street Journal* is indexed in *Predicasts F & S—United States* and in *InfoTrac*, their own index is more thorough. Articles about specific companies are listed in the "Corporate News Section". General business articles are listed in the "General News Section". The Wall Street Journal Index covers the East Coast Edition of the newspaper.

•   PROMT: Predicast's Overview of Markets and Technology (monthly)

This monthly abstracts articles on products, services and industries from 1,200 business and trade publications. Subject index.

•   Index to U.S. Government Periodicals (quarterly)

Provides subject coverage for the articles in 171 government-published journals, most of which are not covered in other indexes. Although this index does not cover articles on specific companies, it is useful for industry information.

•   New York Times Index (semi-monthly)

A detailed index to the *New York Times*. Articles are indexed by subject and name. Each entry includes a brief summary of the article or editorial.

•   Public Affairs Information Service: Bulletin (PAIS) (weekly)

A subject index to current books, pamphlets, periodical articles, and selected government documents. Emphasis is on sources containing factual and statistical information.

•   National Newspaper Index (monthly)

This is an index to articles published in the *Wall Street Journal, Christian Science Monitor, The New York Times, Los Angeles Times,* and *Washington Post*. Published on microfilm, each issue cumulates the entries for the past five years.

THE CARD CATALOG

The card catalog is divided into two sections:
1. Author/Title Catalog—lists books by authors and titles.
2. Subect Catalog—lists the same books by subject.

Using the subject card catalog is a bit more complicated than using the author/title card catalog. If the subject heading needed is not apparent, consult the Library of Congress Subject Headings, a two-volume list of the terms that can be used in the subject card catalog.

MEDIA

MEDIA INFORMATION

The success of a special event depends on the support and coverage by the media. Whether you are searching for a media sponsor or promoting your event, the following sources will make the job much easier.

- **Editor & Publisher International Yearbook (annual)**

This source contains information covering the newspaper industry. Sections include daily newspapers, weekly/special newspapers, Canadian newspapers, newspapers in foreign countries, news and syndicate services, among others. Information given includes address/phone, circulation, special editions, supplements, and management.

- **Broadcasting/Cablecasting Yearbook (annual)**

Published by the Associated Press Broadcasting Services, this source contains information covering the broadcast industry. Indexed by radio and television and cross-referenced by state/province and city. Information given includes format, network affiliate, local/special programming, contacts, address and phone, and group ownership.

- **Gale's Directory of Publications (annual)**

This three-volume directory lists current publications including newspapers, magazines, journals and newsletters. Similar to *Editor and Publisher,* but a more extensive listing. Indexed by state/province and classification (subject).

OTHER SPECIAL EVENT INDUSTRY RESOURCES

The following resources cover a wide range of topics and information relating to special events and corporate sponsorships. They take the form of books, magazines, directories, transcripts and newsletters. The list is not all-inclusive and new sources may appear as quickly as others disappear. Most are not available through your library and you will need to write or call the address/telephone number provided. For most there will be a subscription fee or cost.

(IFEA) INTERNATIONAL FESTIVALS & EVENTS ASSOCIATION

The IFEA is considered the premiere professional organization in the Special Events Industry today and hosts a membership of almost 3,000. Their complete library of resources provides one of the most varied information selections on the industry and covers everything from event planning and preparation to administration and management. They offer the following selections:

- *Festivals (quarterly magazine)*
- *IFEA's Official Guide to Sponsorship*
- *IFEA's Official Guide to Parades*
- *101 Festival Ideas (I Wish I'd Thought Of)*
- *IFEA's Managing Volunteers*
- *IFEA's Producing a Small to Mid-Size Festival*
- *Fundamental Focus*
- *North American Music Festival Directory*
- *Boards That Make A Difference*
- *Special Events: Inside & Out*
- *The Board Development Kit*
- *A Feast of Festivals*
- *BIG E, little e (BIG EVENTS, little events)*
- *Festival & Sponsorship Legal Issues*

- *Event Trends ...In the 90s*
- *IFEA Compensation & Benefits Survey*
- *Parade Management*
- *Creative Event Development*
- *The Key to Success in Running an Outdoor Festival*
- *Money-Making Ideas for Your Event*
- *Creating Special Events*
- *Reinventing Celebration*
- *Multicultural Marketing*
- *Safe & Sound.- A Public Security Handbook*
- *Developing Festival & Event Policy*
- *Event Operations*
- *California Fair & Festival Guide*
- *Building Marketing Alliances*

A variety of educational cassettes are also available upon request. To obtain an order form and/or more complete listing of all materials (including prices), contact the IFEA at (360) 457-3141 or write to: IFEA Library, P.O. Box 2950, Port Angeles, WA 98362.

(IEG) INTERNATIONAL EVENTS GROUP

IEG tracks and analyzes sponsorship of sports, arts, music, causes and events, for the Special Events Industry. They are a specialized source for event marketing publications, sponsorship intelligence and consulting services. Items they offer include:

- *IEG Sponsorship Report™*
- *IEGs Complete Guide to Sponsorship™*
- *IEG Sponsorship Sourcebook™*
- *IEG Legal Guide to Sponsorship™*
- *IEG Consulting™*
- *IEG Sponsordex™/IEG Sponsordex™*
- IEG Marketing Conference™
- IEG Sponsorship Workshop Series ™
- IEG Contracts ™

To obtain an order form and/or more complete listing of all materials (including prices), contact IEG Customer Service at (312) 944-1727.

OTHER RESOURCES

Amusement Business
P.O. Box 24970
Nashville, TN 37202
(615) 321-4250

Arts Management
408 W. 57th Street
New York, NY 10019
(21 2) 245-3850

*Bluegrass Festival
Guide*
Route 5
Kirksville, MO 63501
(816) 665-7172

Chase's Annual Events
180 N. Michigan Ave.
Chicago, IL 60610
(312) 782-9181

*Ernie Saxton's Motor-
sports Sponsorship
Marketing News*
1448 Hollywood Ave.
Langhorne, PA 19047
(215) 752-7797

Events!
6255 Barfield Rd., N.E
Suite 200
Atlanta, GA 30328-9896
1-800-341-9034, ext. 285

*Festival Management
& Event Tourism*
3 Hartsdale Road
Elmsford, NY 10523

*International Council
of Airshows*
1931 Horton Rd., Suite 5
Jackson, MI 49203
(517)782-2424

Arts International
Box 53395
Washington, D.C. 20009
(202) 347-4145

*Aud Arena Stadium
Int'l. Guide*
P.O. Box 24970
Nashville, TN 37202
(615) 321-4250

Brandweek Magazine
P.O. Box 701
Brewster, NY 10509
1-800-722-6658

*EPM Report (Entertain-
ment, Promotion and
Marketing)*
488 E. 1 8th Street
Brooklyn, NY 1 1 226
(718) 469-9330

*Event Management
News*
Beal Publishing
4414 Briarcliff Road, NE
Atlanta, GA 30345
(404) 414-1409

*Fairs & Expositions
Directory*
P.O. Box 985
Springfield, MO 65801
(417) 862-5771

Fireworks Business
Star Route, Box 30
Dingmans Ferry, PA 18325
(717) 828-8417

*International Special
Events Society*
7080 Hollywood Blvd.
Ste. 410
Los Angeles, CA 90028
800-344-ISES

*Music Festivals in
North America*
480 Pleasant St., Suite 5
Lee, MA 10238
(413) 243-0303

Northwest Folklife
305 Harrison St.
Seattle, WA 98109-4695
(206) 684-7300

*Public Relations
Journal*
845 Third Ave.
New York, NY 01122
(212) 826-1766

*Special Events: The Art &
Science of Celebration*
Goldblatt & Associates
807 Davis Dr.
Brentwood, TN 37210

Sponsorship News
P.O. Box 66
Wokingham Berkshire
RG41 5FS ENGLAND
01 734-772770

Sports Market Place
P.O. Box 1417
Princeton, NJ 08542
(609) 921-8599

*Music Festivals
in Europe*
Berkshire Traveller Press
480 Pleasant St., Suite 5
Lee, MA 10238
(413) 243-0303

*O'Dwyer's Directory of
P.R. Firms*
271 Madison Ave.
New York, NY 10016
(212) 826-1766

*Road Race Manage-
ment Newsletter*
4904 Glen Cove
Parkway
Bethesda, MD 20816
(301) 320-6865

Sponsors Report
3785 Varsity Dr.
Ann Arbor, MI 48108
(313) 971-1900

*Sponsorship Principles
& Practices*
Ron Bergin & Assoc.
PO Box 6487
Evanston, IL 60202
(609)921-8599

*Stern's Performing Arts
Directory*
33 W. 60th St. 10th Floor
New York, NY 10023
(212) 245-9050

CHAPTER NINE

THE STRATEGY OF SELLING

In his book, *A Kick In the Seat of the Pants,* Roger Von Oech talks about using the explorer, judge, artist, and warrior roles to generate and implement ideas. So far, the explorer has done the research, the judge has analyzed the event, and the artist has creatively transformed information into new ideas. Now it is time to become the warrior so that ideas can be carried into action.

The warrior realizes that there are many obstacles and much competition along the path to success. Primarily, however, the warrior knows that by taking the offensive and planning a proper strategy, chances for success are high.

Good warriors, be they generals or foot soldiers, would never go into battle without proper support. In the case of selling, this support comes from the research and positioning discussed thus far. To begin selling without these elements of support greatly diminishes the likelihood of success.

With support in place, attention can be turned to the strategy of selling. In planning strategy, a number of factors must be considered: pricing, sales meetings, proposals, and sponsor service.

THE ELUSIVE EVENT-PRICING FORMULA

One of the few certainties in the field of special events is that there is uncertainty in how to price them. There are no rate cards as there are in advertising. Traditionally, sponsorships have been priced arbitrarily, depending on what the market will bear, but that is changing as sponsors become more experienced and sophisticated.

Sponsorship is not a new game to most companies anymore, especially not to those that have been the major targets of events seeking support. Very few sponsors walk blindly into supporting an event. At one time, event marketers could approach potential sponsors, tell them title sponsorship cost $50,000, and the sponsor would have to take it or leave it. Some price differences among similar events were simply due to different salespeople. Now, more sophisticated sponsors are saying, "This is the value we place on that and this is what we are willing to pay."

Many larger companies and agencies with sponsorship experience have created entire rating systems to help them remove the subjective side of the process and decide with which events to become associated. (See Chapter Ten.) As event sponsorship continues to grow, that trend will catch on with smaller companies.

While there remains no standard pricing formula that applies to all events, the following principles may be helpful.

Sponsors see events as a less expensive way than purchasing conventional advertising to reach targeted marketing goals. In most instances, events should not try or expect to get the same amount of dollars as companies pay for print or broadcast media campaigns.

The simplest way to price an event is to break it down into its component parts. If it's a football game, for instance, there might be a pre-game show, the game itself, a halftime show, and

possibly a post-game show. Add up the actual costs of the components, including administration and overhead, and then add a "value cost" that accounts for the fact that the event wouldn't exist without the school, association, or organization that is hosting it. In some instances, it is desirable to turn a profit on the event; under other circumstances, it is appropriate only to cover costs and to ensure no loss of funds.

The total of the component costs plus the value costs is the total cost for the event, and sponsorship prices can be obtained from that figure. For instance, if the game costs $10,000, a title sponsorship could go for $5,000 dollars and five co-sponsorships could go for $1,000 each. Components can be sold separately or together as one event. *Event* costs should increase annually by five to ten percent or by the actual cost of doing the event.

For buying into an event, of course, sponsors will expect to get something in return, such as publicity, customer/client/employee hospitality opportunities through free tickets or pre-game parties, direct sales or sampling opportunities during the game, or a positive image by providing tickets to a local charity. *The make-up of each sponsorship package will depend on the objectives of each sponsor. The sponsorship pricing formula should include the cost of these benefits.*

Another pricing method is having sponsors guarantee no losses. *If the only concern, as we mentioned earlier, is not to lose money, the best approach to a sponsor may be an agreement whereby the company guarantees to help the event break even* by covering any non-recovered costs.

Using the football game example again, if it takes $10,000 to break even and $8,000 in revenue is collected, then the sponsor pays the $2,000 difference. The event is guaranteed not to lose money and the sponsor (as the event underwriter) will not have to pay a dime to attach its name to the event if the event makes money or at least breaks even.

Those selling sponsorships, especially for first-time events, should start the relationship with potential sponsors slowly. It's important not to be too greedy just because the sign on the door says Coca-Cola or IBM. Some think that just because a company is large, it can afford to pay more for a sponsorship. While this may be true, the bottom line is this: from a company's perspective, higher prices mean higher returns. Company representatives will expect more value and will know what to ask for in terms of exposure.

It is often worthwhile to make the price very reasonable for a major sponsor just to get that sponsor involved. This is especially true for newer events that are still being scrutinized. A major sponsors adds credibility.

Most companies will not sponsor an event with one of their competitors. *Determine exclusivity patterns before approaching potential sponsors.* Is it better to go after Coca-Cola or Pepsi? Will XYZ Appliance come aboard if ABC Appliance is a sponsor?

If possible, don't quote a price; quote a range. Every sponsor has different goals end objectives, and there should be a package for everyone. Although guidelines are important, don't be so rigid that potential sponsors are lost. *Package the elements of a sponsorship.* Don't nickel-and-dime a sponsor to death by continuing to add options that increase the price. "All-inclusive" and "turn-key" events are very desirable to companies without large staffs or budgets.

Find out what resources a company offers besides cash. Some sponsors may not be in a position to pay large cash sponsorship fees but may be willing to offer products or in-kind services, such as airline tickets, hotel rooms, car rentals, or advertising that can help decrease the event's operating expenses.

Sponsors should expect to pay premium prices for title or exclusive sponsorship or for the right to be the "official" product or service of an event. Also, if an event has a successful track record, sponsors should be willing to pay a higher price to become associated with it. Future sales efforts make it important to document everything about the event, particularly attendance and media coverage. (See Chapter Eleven.)

FACE TO FACE: SPONSORSHIP SALES MEETINGS

In almost every case, the most desirable initial contact with a prospective sponsor is a personal visit; this is often easier said than done. Before phoning to make an appointment, check available research information to ensure calling the proper person in the organization. The basic rule of thumb is to start as high on the corporate ladder as possible. Preferably, meet with a person who has the authority to make decisions on the type of sponsorship and dollar level being proposed.

If asked the purpose of the meeting be prepared to offer a brief description. Too much detail, however, often results in a "no, thanks" or, almost as undesirable, a "send me something in the mail" response.

Tenacity is a prerequisite for a successful salesperson, and sponsorship sales require the most tenacious salespeople. Perseverance in just the right amount brings success. Make buddies with their secretaries; get them on your side. These gatekeepers hold the magic key to who gets time with those they guard so well. An even better route is to find someone else who can open the door to the target, e.g., a member of the board, another sponsor, or a relative.

If still unable to secure a personal meeting, go ahead and send the material with a cover letter requesting an audience. One or two weeks later, make a follow-up call asking if the material was received and again request a meeting. If the response is negative, remove the company from the candidate list—until next year. By then, a successful event this year may have made the opportunity more attractive.

Once initial obstacles are overcome, the sales meeting can take place. Be aware that, unlike many typical sales situations, sponsorships are rarely agreed upon at the initial meeting; follow-up is required to work out all the details and secure a signed agreement. These guidelines can help ensure a successful outcome to the sales meeting:

Be prepared

Have homework and research done. Go into the meeting with a well-thought-out proposal in mind, but leave enough flexibility to change directions if necessary and appropriate.

Be on time

Running late will frustrate both seller and sponsor, and it will limit the valuable time needed to present the proposal.

Include others with influence

Have one or two extremely well-prepared event board or committee members or current sponsors present at all meetings with potential sponsors at major levels. Each should be thoroughly familiar with every aspect of the event and its benefits relative to the potential sponsor's objectives.

Include a familiar representative

If possible, one of those present should know the sponsor representative personally or professionally.

Include someone with expert knowledge

If any one objective is perceived to be a primary company objective, include a staff or event board member who can cover that area thoroughly in the meeting.

Be enthusiastic

As any good salesperson knows, enthusiasm is essential in successful selling. Everyone in the meeting should possess and display sincere enthusiasm for what they are selling.

Help determine sponsor objectives

Be prepared to assist the potential sponsor with determining objectives his or her company should meet through sponsor participation. Surprisingly, too many companies frequently do not know what they really want or how they can benefit from such programs. Gentle guidance can often produce positive results for both the sponsor-seeker and the company.

Create urgency

The "feeling" and "atmosphere" of a meeting will determine whether this next tactic should be taken: without threatening intent, do mention in the meeting that other sponsors are being sought. If there are set prices for sponsorships or a limited number of sponsorships, indicate chat selection will be on a first-come, first-served basis. If prices are negotiable, so state, but indicate diplomatically that the best offer will be taken. This must be done smoothly.

Control the length of the meeting

Unless the atmosphere and conversation dictate otherwise, plan to limit this initial meeting to

30 minutes and promise chat limitation in the initial phone call.

Follow-up

Determine follow-up actions to be taken by everyone involved, and arrange a follow-up meeting if necessary.

Set a decision date

Try to determine a target date for a decision, take note of it, and call on or about that date if the company has not made contact by that time.

Emphasize the convenience of sponsorship

Illustrate clearly that the entire event under consideration is totally self-contained and can function with as little labor and time commitment as the sponsor wishes.

Aside of, or along with cost, the most often given reason for rejection is fear of labor and time intensity. Most staff members who would be involved on behalf of the sponsoring entity feel they already have too much to do and simply cannot handle additional work, especially something as big and time-involved as an event. A few like to get heavily involved once they get going and see how much fun it is. However, initial clearance and periodic review of progress is all the time and attention chat should be required of sponsors.

THE PERFECT PROPOSAL

At some point in the sponsorship search, a newcomer will first hear those most famous of lines, "Send it to me in writing." It is at this point that he or she will join the ranks of just about everyone else in the industry in the age-old quest for the "perfect" proposal. If we may share years of searching and help minimize frustration, it is with this bit of wisdom chat won't come as a surprise to anyone, "There is no such thing as a perfect proposal."

Studies done in research for this book, as well as others done by the International Events Group, suggest a number of interesting interpretations by those representing both events and sponsors, but conclusions have not yet been drawn as to the best way to create proposals. In fact, there are as many approaches to writing proposals as there are events and sponsors. The "perfect" proposal is the one that works. However, there are always ways to improve proposals. What follows are a few basics that seem to work in most situations.

First and foremost, learn to write!

A proposal full of poor grammar, basic punctuation errors, and typos will not fare very well. Local community colleges and other educational institutions offer a variety of classes in basic grammatical rules, writing for business, creative writing, and even writing proposals. Investment of time and dollars in such classes will reap many benefits down the road.

Proposals must be reasonable in length

Whatever is included must be pertinent to each particular sponsor and proposal. Most sponsors read many proposals daily and do not have time to wade through volumes of information in each one. The result: they may not read it at all. A sponsor contact with a major food company tells us that he once received a proposal that weighed nearly five pounds!

Try not to send generic proposals

Use information obtained from research to personalize each proposal as much as possible. At least make a phone call and ask questions regarding the sponsor's goals and objectives. Gear the proposal to meet their needs. Read through their annual reports and other in-house sources, and look for terminology that can be built into a proposal. This will indicate that you know what you're talking about and to whom you're talking. Appeal to the receiver's needs in all cases. Say what they want to hear.

Develop a professional presentation

You wouldn't go to a business meeting wearing torn blue jeans and a faded T-shirt; don't send your proposal that way, either! Neatness and appearance count. Typos, binding, grammar and the quality of your support materials can make or break a proposal. Remember Tom Peters' "Toilets 101" theory mentioned earlier? If the proposal and materials are poorly presented, what will the event be like?

Remember: timing, timing, timing

One of the gravest, often fatal, mistakes sponsor-seekers make is allowing too little time between their initial approach and the start of the event. Company representatives must have time to study and discuss thoroughly the pros and cons of each seriously considered proposal. If they like the proposal, they must then sell it to management, find funding, set up any needed staff participation, and so forth.

A primary consideration in terms of timing is the prospect's fiscal year. Normally, corporations need four to six months to prepare for the coming fiscal year—to determine goals, set up budgets, define staff numbers and any reassignments, etc. Strong efforts should be made to approach major sponsorship candidates three to four months ahead of the beginning of the fiscal year in which the sponsorship is to be expended.

SUGGESTED PROPOSAL LAYOUT

While we have admitted there is no such thing as a perfect proposal, we would be remiss if we did not provide a basic outline for those who are just beginning in the event sponsorship arena. Hopefully, this will also help pros crystallize their thinking.

The following, based on discussions with a number of professionals representing both events and sponsors, is meant to be a guideline for an effective sponsorship proposal. As you read, develop new ideas and concepts. Try new approaches; don't get deaf to only one way of doing anything.

"The yellow pad is the blank canvas of the businessman."   — Bill Ghormley

---

SPONSORSHIP PROPOSAL FORMAT

Executive Summary

The executive summary can be sent with the full proposal or on its own with a cover letter. The summary should be a maximum of two pages in length and should represent a condensed proposal, including the following:

1. Introduction
2. Opportunities/Benefits
3. Investment
4. Deadline

Situation Appraisal

This covers a brief explanation of why the event exists, using "subliminal ties" to the interests, goals, and objectives of the potential sponsor, i.e. quotes and terminology taken from their annual report.

Event Background and Track Record

This includes a brief history of the event along with information about its successful involvement with similar sponsors.

Proposal and Benefits

This is what the event is proposing the sponsor provide and what the benefits will be in return.

Investment

This is just another word for "cost," but it sounds much better. This section will detail the company's expenditures for the project.

Deadline for Decision

The date for the company's final response should be stated explicitly herein.

Addenda

Support materials, press clippings that include the names of sponsors, letters of recommendation, and other indications of success can be included in this section.

SPONSOR SERVICE

Selling sponsorship is really a two-part topic:

1.   How to *attract* a sponsor
2.   How to *keep* a sponsor

Unfortunately, not enough people think about the second part. Superior sponsor service, once the contract is signed, is the first step toward selling them on future participation. Sponsors must trust you, respect you and like you. This can only come from integrity demonstrated over time.

A true account: one event administrator talks about an event that was very successful in every way; when the time came to evaluate the event, however, the thing that stuck with the sponsor was that an event staff member had left a typewriter turned on over a weekend at the sponsor's office and had thus caused an employee to complain! "Little things mean a lot."

There are a few helpful tips that can keep problems to a minimum.

Don't over-promise; over-deliver

Don't promise the impossible to make a sale. One overzealous salesperson promised in a proposal to Wheaties to double their sales! Obviously, this person did not do enough research.

Designate a contact person

Always have a point person once an agreement is signed. The sponsor should never have to search for answers or help. By having one contact person for each sponsor, a great deal of confusion and aggravation can be avoided.

Respect the sponsor's time

Whether in a meeting or on the phone, assume the sponsor has other things to do. Ask if you are calling at a convenient moment, etc.

Respond to turn-downs

Even though a negative answer is not fun to receive, thank potential sponsors for a prompt response and leave a positive door open for the future. Allow them to get out of things comfortably and they'll be sold more easily the next time.

Keep in touch

Communicate with sponsors even when they're not needed. Potential sponsors shouldn't think every call is a request for cash. Two or three years down the road, the relationship could pay off.

~ CHAPTER TEN ~

SPONSORSHIP: A CORPORATE VIEW

The companies and organizations, for whom the sponsor-seekers have been analyzing, researching, positioning, and readying their best proposals, may need some help of their own. The success of corporate sponsorship, along with a decrease in government support of many nonprofit programs, has opened a floodgate of sponsor-seekers and events, all of which believe they have the answer to every possible marketing or public relations objective that a potential sponsor may have. A line forms for every available dollar.

This onslaught of proposals and the perceived need to jump into the sponsorship game with competitors and peers has forced some businesses to place the "special events" title and function on both individuals and departments that are ill equipped to handle this function properly. It is as important for the corporate sector to prepare and evaluate its methods and goals for handling special events as it is for events personnel to do so.

Some of today's top companies are surprisingly unsophisticated in their approach to and processing of sponsorship proposals. This is partially due to sheer numbers, as many large companies receive thousands of proposals each year. Of those, many are not suitable to the company's needs, and the rest usually don't work out for one reason or another. This leads many companies to consider creating their own events. (See Chapter Three.)

TIPS OF THE TRADE

For those businesses and organizations considering sponsorship, the following tips will help make life a little easier:

Do not lead on a sponsor-seeker

A polite and prompt decision, even a negative one, will be appreciated, and this will often stop persistent follow-up efforts.

Consider every proposal fairly

Assuming that no one knows what you need may cause you to miss that once-in-a-lifetime opportunity. At least give sponsor-seekers the courtesy of actually looking at their proposals. One major soft drink bottler replied to a questionnaire (not a proposal) for this book with an unsigned form letter saying that the company appreciated our proposal but that we didn't fit into the budget. Obviously, this respondent did not even look at our information long enough to send an intelligent response.

Be Courteous

A friendly mailer or computer letter is acceptable, but it should show real consideration of a proposed event and sincere appreciation that the event organizers thought to offer the company the opportunity to consider involvement. Phone calls to more major events will be appreciated. Remember, down the road, today's "Nos" may have an event you would love to be a part of, and you will want them to think of you again.

Investigate opportunities

When seriously interested in a proposal's opportunities, thoroughly investigate. Ask for:

- Details of the event's operational history

- Sponsorship fee history

- Names of previous and present sponsors

- Event demographics and psychographics

- Background of the event organizers

- Event competition and "look-alikes"

- Specifics of the event contract

- Expert appraisal of new event potential and "ambush marketing" possibilities

EVALUATING SERIOUS-CANDIDATE PROPOSALS

Many sponsorships are entered into emotionally. While emotion need not totally be removed from the sponsorship decision process, other factors must be weighed to ensure that a responsible choice is made. An "Evaluation Profile Sheet" can enable a more objective appraisal.

An Evaluation Profile Sheet

- Must be individualized to a specific company's goals and objectives

- Provides a graphic or numerical picture of an event's potential

- Does not measure one sponsorship opportunity against another

- Can help sell an event to higher-ups

- Might help stem executive privilege in event selection

- Becomes a tool by which to evaluate the success of an event

We have provided below descriptions of the criteria that can be utilized in the evaluation process. These are followed by one example of an "Evaluation Profile Sheet."

EVALUATION CRITERIA

Publicity

Has the event magnetized considerable publicity in the past? What was the nature of that publicity? Will it reach the right media and market segments for this company? Does it have potential to be made "fresh" to attract more coverage?

Direct Product Sales Potential

Are there opportunities to sell, sample, or distribute coupons for the product at the event? Is proof-of-purchase for admission permitted and appropriate? Are there other types of methods offered by the event for direct product sales, such as using the product in the event?

Image Agreement

How well does this event fit our established (or new) image? Does it mesh with a current or upcoming advertising theme? Is it of the quality that compares with this company's reputation?

Other Sponsors

Who are they? Are there any competitors? Are others of an image that would make them "good companions" for our company? Is this a tide sponsorship for us or for some other company? How important is it for more public credit to be given to us than to other firms?

Event History

Is it an established event? If so, has it had good reaction in the past from its audiences? Have there been any problems of any kind? Who were previous sponsors? Is it tired? Can it be freshened up?

Event Potential

How important is it that this is a new event? Can it be an effective project if it is planned as a one-time presentation? Is it likely to grow if it is to become a regular event? What can we expect in the way of increasing sponsorship costs in the future?

Event "Deal"

How valuable is the total package being offered? Would we be buying more than we need because the event influence is well beyond our territory? Can advertising, public relations, or other marketing elements do a better job for this amount of money? Can the producers really deliver what they claim? Can they deliver what we want?

Implementation Demands

How easy is it to put this show on the road? Will it require and tie up too many of our personnel? Will any voluntary assistance be required? If so, how much, and from where will we get it? Is the event easily do-able?

Return on Investment

This is a general, personal assessment that takes all of the above into consideration but permits a very subjective "I like it," or "I don't like it" based on intuition.

More than one person should be given an evaluation sheet for each event being considered because assessments are highly subjective. Note: This method may be used to evaluate and compare results among many events, or to let each sheet or summary of several sheets provide a numerical value for a single event. This allows decision makers to see how closely it fits the company's needs.

Evaluation Profile Sheet for Candidate Sponsorship												
Criteria	Value Categories	Comparative Ratings										
		10	20	30	40	50	60	70	80	90	100	
PUBLICITY APPRAISAL	Objective											
	Event											
DIRECT PRODUCT SELL	Objective											
	Event											
IMAGE AGREEMENT	Objective											
	Event											
OTHER SPONSORS	Objective											
	Event											
EVENT HISTORY	Objective											
	Event											
EVENT POTENTIAL	Objective											
	Event											
EVENT "DEAL"	Objective											
	Event											
IMPLEMENTATION DEMANDS	Objective											
	Event											
RETURN-ON INVESTMENT JUDGMENT	Objective											
	Event											

■ SECTION 3 ■

EVALUATION:
MEASURING SPONSORSHIP EFFECTIVENESS

CHAPTER ELEVEN

ALL'S WELL THAT ENDS WELL

The evaluation process is perhaps the most debated topic in the events industry today. The questions of who should evaluate, what should be evaluated and how to evaluate accurately have all been answered with a plethora of opinions and approaches. Still, there remains a void when it comes to any established and accepted industry standards. This is partially due to the disparities among the events and sponsors that comprise the events industry. This differs from the industrywide similarities shared by those in conventional marketing fields.

WHY EVALUATE?

While exact industry standards have not yet been set, there is agreement on the significance of evaluation. Evaluation serves a number of important purposes to both event personnel and sponsors. It should not be perceived as a single step in the sponsorship process but rather as an ongoing procedure throughout all steps.

In evaluating events, event personnel should:

- determine where the event can add strengths or replace weaknesses;
- determine what is currency offered and how other opportunities for potential sponsors can be added;
- determine successes and failures within current sponsorships; and

- secure accurate statistics that will help sell and re-sell future sponsorships.

In evaluating events, sponsors should:

- determine corporate goals and objectives;
- determine whether potential event sponsorships meet corporate goals and objectives; and
- determine successes and failures of current sponsorships.

The first two purposes for both event personnel and sponsors were covered in Chapters 7 and 10 and are internal functions. In this section we will look more closely at the evaluation that takes place once a sponsorship agreement is in place.

WHO SHOULD EVALUATE?

While there are many opinions regarding who should bear the responsibility for evaluating a particular event, we believe that a good evaluation must come from both sides of the fence. Because the information gained from an effective evaluation will benefit both the event and the sponsor, agreement about what benchmarks success will be judged against, the most effective methods for securing this information, and who can most effectively oversee this process should be reached early.

In many cases, it may be most effective to hire an outside firm to secure and analyze the necessary information for evaluation, thus removing any staffing burdens or prejudices that may affect the process. Many independent sponsorship research companies are better equipped with the tools necessary to analyze data, especially media coverage, and present it in an easy-to-understand format.

For those whose budgets do not allow this approach, evaluation can still be accomplished in-house in cost-effective ways.There is no excuse for not evaluating at all, but sponsors say that nine out of ten events never do any type of evaluation with them. The cost of not evaluating may prove far greater in the long run.

WHAT SHOULD YOU EVALUATE?

There are three "musts" in measuring sponsorship:

• Have specific objectives
• Measure where the company stands against those objectives at the outset of the sponsorship
• Use those objectives as benchmarks to evaluate the success of the sponsorship

For sponsors, objectives should coincide with those established on the Evaluation Profile Sheet in Chapter Ten. For events, two sets of objectives should be established: generic and specific.

Generic objectives are those that help sell future sponsorships.These include:

• Attendance
• Demographic Reach
• Media Coverage
• Cash Intake

Specific objectives are those directly aimed at individual sponsors; these help sell or keep current sponsorships.To arrive at these objectives, sit down with your sponsors and determine what their specific objectives are. (See Chapter One.) Companies new to event sponsorship may need some help and direction in setting their objectives.

In response to a survey done for this book, both sponsors and events were asked to identify the most common methods of evaluation.These are listed in order of popularity, not necessarily in order of ability to provide reliable indications of success or failure:

1. Media Impressions
2. Attendance
3. Product Sales or Sampling

HOW SHOULD EVALUATIONS BE DONE?

Marketers and sponsors who know what they are doing know that the right sponsorships work; proving it, however, is difficult. This fact must be faced. However, according to the IEG Sponsorship Report, such marketing experts as Anheuser-Busch, Coca-Cola, Pepsi, RJR Nabisco, and 4,000 plus other companies combined will spend more than $5.9 billion dollars on sponsorship fees alone (not including support of those sponsorships, advertising, public relations or promotions) in 1997. They would not spend that kind of money if they did not know that sponsorships work.

Event marketing does work, but it is very hard to measure.We will cover a few basic measurements used in evaluation and suggest methods for collecting this information.The important thing is that the methodology used to evaluate should be consistent with the goals being evaluated.

MEASUREMENTS AND METHODS

Audience Count

Attendance is one of the simplest things to measure in a controlled situation, and this is most accurately done through ticket sales, turnstile counts, or established seating capacities. In a noncontrolled situation, estimates from law enforcement agencies, parks and recreation departments, or other organizations involved in crowd control are usually reliable. Broadcast audience reach figures are obtainable from the station or network providing coverage. Counts by event producers alone are often suspect, however.

Surveys or Polls

These are usually done by an outside company that specializes in the field. Surveys or polls can be done over the telephone, via direct mail, or in person during the event. Surveys or polls usually provide good data about whether a targeted market has been reached and what the "perceptions" of a particular event or sponsor are. A combination of pre- and post-tests can help determine whether changes in these areas were due directly to a particular event.

Media Impressions and Publicity

Publicity can be measured by counting sponsor- or event-specific mentions and multiplying them by the appropriate circulation or number of viewers and listeners to come up with combined media impressions. Many sponsors attempt to improve this measure by ranking the type of coverage (e.g., the name in the headline or a photo vs. a mention in the text) and the value of where it was received (e.g., Vogue vs. Time). However, efforts to quantify the true value of publicity and put a yardstick to the quality of such mentions are, for the most part, futile.

Advertising Space

Advertising space mentioning the sponsor or event may be figured at a value equal to the purchase price of that advertising. Many sponsors attempt to calculate the percentage of direct name mention (location, size, and length of mention within an advertisement) as opposed to the value of an entire advertisement. Sponsors often require ad approval to ensure best name placement.

Product Sales, Sampling, and Couponing

These are easily tallied and are, perhaps, the only truly meaningful measurements of direct sponsorship success.

Image Skew

Quantifying changes in image, attitudes created, perceptions changed or associations suggested is extremely difficult. While surveys and polls are the best methods for obtaining such information, most sponsors with these ethereal objectives understand the inherent difficulties and "measure" their success by comments they hear, smiles they see, etc.

WHEN SHOULD YOU EVALUATE?

Evaluation is an ongoing process, but the most crucial time to evaluate an event is immediately after it is over. It is essential to do a prompt evaluation session with all sponsors while things are still fresh in everyone's mind. This evaluation can be either written or oral and is preferably a combination of the two.

Evaluating the goals and objectives determined at the start of the sponsorship agreement during this session will help highlight the positives and diffuse any negatives by dealing with them promptly. It also allows the foundation to be laid for repeat sponsorship. It is advisable to give sponsors a gift of some type that will help keep the event foremost in their minds. A framed photo or poster, a video tape highlighting the sponsor's involvement, or another keepsake memento can be worth more sponsorship support later down the road.

■ SECTION 4 ■

THE SPECIAL EVENTS INDUSTRY: TODAY AND TOMORROW

Chapter Twelve

WHAT'D THEY SAY?

The future of the special events industry is very bright. In the years ahead there will be increased growth, greater opportunities, and continued fine tuning of what we have learned so far. There will also be new challenges to be met and new demands on our creativity.

In an effort to take a sampling of the special events industry today, we questioned 100 organizations representing both events and sponsors of all sizes. The following are conclusions drawn from that information. Some conclusions differ from points made elsewhere in this book, and both should be considered in formulating your own opinion. A different or larger sampling might yield different results.

PEOPLE AND PAY

Those just entering the special events industry are joining a very diverse group of individuals. The events side is divided fairly evenly between men and women and has an average age span of 40 to 50. The majority are college educated, and many have advanced degrees. Their degrees run the gamut from criminology to anthropology and from journalism to sports management, although there is a new lean toward business management and related marketing, personnel and public relations emphases, in the absence of a formal special events degree program. Thanks to new efforts in our field, this void will soon begin to be filled.

The corporate side leans much more heavily to men (80 percent), with the average age span re-

maining 40 to 50. Again, most are college graduates, but fewer have advanced or graduate degrees. For the most part their degrees are in business-oriented areas, such as marketing, management, communications, and public relations.

Forty-five percent of those in the special events industry, across both groups, have between six and ten years experience. Another 20 percent have 11 to 15 years of experience. Those with less than five years' experience represent the lowest numbers and perhaps are a cause for concern over new blood and fresh ideas in the years ahead.

On the corporate side of the industry, 80 percent of event managers who responded earn over $50,000 per year, and 50 percent earn over $60,000. Sixty percent of their staffs earn between $31,000 and $40,000 yearly.

Event management averaged between $41,000 and $50,000 with a respectable 54 percent earning over $40,000 per year. Seventy percent of their staffs earned between $21,000 and $40,000 yearly.

Corporations currently employ an average of two full-time and one part-time employees to deal with events and event sponsorship. Events have an average of 2.1 full-time and 1.2 part-time employees. Most do not plan to add any additional staff in the next five years, but no one plans to decrease staff. Of those who do plan to add, who will they add?

Corporations hope to add sales and marketing and support staff. Events hope to add production staff, sales and marketing staff, promotion staff, support staff, and consultants, in that order.

WHAT'S IN A TITLE?

As special events are still relatively new to the corporate structure, a variety of departments have been given responsibility for overseeing the event marketing function. According to our findings, the most common are:

- Marketing
- Public Relations
- Event Marketing
- Advertising
- Promotions

At the same time, a variety of titles have been created for those persons in charge. Among them are:

- Vice President of any/all of the Above Departments
- Director of Public Relations/Event Marketing
- Director of Special Promotions
- Director of Event Management
- Manager of Merchandising
- Special Projects Manager
- Corporate Accounts Manager
- Manager of Community Relations

CAUSE-RELATED MARKETING

A great majority of today's events are non-profit operations. This allows many corporations to combine marketing dollars with charitable or foundation dollars to sponsor events, although fewer are doing so, distinguishing between events and causes. Thirty-seven percent of events claim to be cause-related, but those causes are neither politically or religiously oriented in 92 percent of the cases. This may reflect the fact that 90 percent of those corporations questioned will not sponsor events with those ties.

The most interesting cause to sponsors today? Children/Education. Likely causes of tomorrow? Health issues, education, children, the homeless, and the environment.

IMPACT TARGETS

More sponsors (60 percent) prefer larger events with many impressions to smaller events with potentially higher quality impressions (25 percent). The remainder have no preference.

A lean toward more targeted marketing is obvious, as 65 percent of the sponsors said they preferred events with a local impact, 25 percent preferred regional activities, and 10 percent opted for national events. By comparison, event personnel most often thought their projects had regional impact (63 percent). The fewest respondents (17 percent) considered their event's impact to be national.

The majority of events and sponsorships take place during the summer, followed by spring, fall, and winter, respectively.

What is the average target market for corporate sponsors?

- Age: 37
- Sex: Male/Female
- Income: $36,400 per household
- Education: High School plus
- Lifestyle: Urban/Rural

Note: More sponsors are going after general across the board target markets and families.

What is the average event audience member?

- Age: 36
- Sex: 50% male; 50% female
- Income: $38,800 per household
- Education: High School plus
- Lifestyle: Urban

Note: Events have also taken greater aim at broad target markets and families.

BUDGET

Those answering for companies indicated that an average of 22 percent of their marketing budgets are spent on event sponsorship and an average of 57 percent is spent on conventional advertising. On the average, they project that in five years the budget share will decrease to 17.5 percent for events, this will be offset by an increase to 66 percent for conventional advertising. Producing tangible results may reverse this trend in favor of events.

The average dollar amount spent annually on event marketing by sponsors was over $1 million, with an average of $55,000 per event.

An average of 8.1 percent of an event's budget is set aside for sponsor relations.

Both groups agreed that approximately 75 percent of their sponsorships are paid in cash and 25 percent are paid via tradeout agreements for products, services, etc. Corporations and events both place, on an average, a two-to-one ratio on trade-out value versus cash.

BENEFITS

What do events and sponsors believe are the major factors (top 10) that corporate sponsors look for in an event?

Sponsors	Events
1. Total Audience	Sales/Sampling
2. Sponsor Service/Follow-Through	Hospitality Opportunities
3. Sponsorship Fee	Media Coverage
4. Other Sponsors	Signage
5. Name in Event Title	Association with Event
6. Event History/Success	Event Demographics
7. Right-of-first refusal	Networking with Other sponsors
8. Signage	Advertising Package
9. Media Coverage	Total Exposure
10. Category Exclusivity	Employee participation

PROPOSALS AND PRICING

How many proposals do corporations actually receive? Of those we asked, the estimated averages were 5.7 per week, 11.6 per month, and 149 per year. There are extremes on both ends. How many proposals do events send? Those queried estimated an average of 4.6 per week, 11 per month, and 84.3 per year.

Sponsors prefer to receive proposals that are personalized every time, but they actually receive 63 percent that are generic and 37 percent that are personalized. One hundred percent want prices included in the proposal. Of event planners, on the other hand, 90 percent prefer to personalize proposals, and 10 percent prefer generic proposals. They actually send 86 percent personalized and 14 percent generic. Eighty-five percent include prices in their proposals.

According to sponsors, these are the elements of an effective proposal (not in specific order):

- Other Sponsors
- Target Audience Demographics and Psychographics
- Cost
- Benefits
- Brevity
- History/Track Record/Attendance
- Budget/Profit Disbursement (if any)
- Neatness/Clarity
- Long Lead Time (Note: Most sponsors list a January-December fiscal budget year)
- Personalization
- Event Overview/Dates

According to event staffs, effective proposals include the following (not in specific order):

- Demographics
- Benefits
- Cost (Levels)
- Event Description/Overview
- Introduction/Executive Summary
- Exposure
- Sponsor Promotional Opportunities
- Other and Past Sponsors
- History and Track Record
- Personalization
- Support Materials

What are the top three complaints that sponsors have regarding Incoming proposals?

1.   Not personalized
2.   No appreciation of Business—haven't researched corporate objectives
3.   Costs exceed value

What about the top three complaints that events have regarding corporate handling of proposals?

1.   Extreme delay in decision-making process
2.   No response at all
3.   Benefits expected exceed sponsorship provided

What is the average dollar amount requested in proposals?

According to sponsors:
35%	$ 11,000 - $ 50,000
30%	$ 5,000 - $ 10,000
20%	$ 57,000 - $100,000
10%	under $5,000
5%	$101,000 - $500,000

According to events:

35%	$11,000 - $ 50,000
31%	$ 5,000 - $ 10,000
28%	under $5,000
5%	$51,000 - $100,000

Sponsors reported that they received 68 proposals to every one they used. Event personnel said they sent out six proposals for every one that was accepted.

CONTACT AND FOLLOW-UP

The majority of sponsors prefer initial contact be made by mail and follow-up contacts be made by phone. Events prefer both to be by phone or in person.

If interested in an event, 100 percent of sponsors said they respond by telephone. If not, 80 percent respond by mail, 10 percent by phone, and 10 percent do not respond at all, especially if it is a generic proposal.

Corporate respondents to the question of the most effective way for potential event marketers to approach them indicated the following order of preference:

1.   Networking through peers
2.   Targeted Research
3.   Direct Mail
4.   Personal Relationship/Meeting
5.   Telemarketing
6.   Advertisements
7.   Trade Shows/Seminars

Which approaches do events use most?

1.   Networking
2.   Targeted Research
3.   Direct Mail
4.   Trade Shows/Seminars
5.   Telemarketing
6.   Advertising

Asked how often they keep in touch with sponsors between sponsorships, events responded as follows:

- 14% Annually
- 18% Bi-annually
- 42% Monthly
- 26% Other

How do they keep in touch?

- 85% by telephone
- 76% by letter
- 52% by newsletter
- 40% in person, or other

EVALUATION AND MEASUREMENT

Who measures the success of a particular event or sponsorship?

Ninety percent of the sponsors questioned said that they did, 70 percent of the event people said that they did.

Who should measure?

Most events and sponsors agreed that a good evaluation is the responsibility of both event and sponsor. Even though there are outside agencies that specialize in evaluation, the large majority of events and sponsors keep this function in-house.

How much do they spend on this important function?

Sponsors spend an average of 1.5 percent of their event marketing budget, events an average of 1 percent of their budget on evaluation.

RESEARCH AND PROSPECTING

How much time do events spend researching potential sponsors?

An average of 15 percent of working hours was indicated.

What are the best sources of information available on these respective entities?

Corporate sponsors say the best ways to find out about them are via annual reports, media coverage, their public relations department, advertising journals, and by making a simple phone call.

Events say the best sources of information on their own organizations include their marketing packet, their event program, brochure, or video, the *IEG Sponsorship Source Book*, the *International Festivals and Events Association Directory*, media coverage, and by making a simple phone call.

How do potential sponsors research an event?

1. Networking with other sponsors/peers
2. Market research
3. Professional event sources

GENERAL DATA

Who makes most corporate sponsorship decisions?

According to those we questioned, most are made by upper management (60 percent), followed by committee (25 percent), and lastly by one individual (15%).

What is the average turnaround time for a sponsorship decision?

Two to three months.

What percentage of the time do companies create their own events vs. sponsoring existing events?

- 33% Create their own
- 67% Sponsor existing events

STATE OF THE ART

For fun, we asked both sponsors and events to pick their top choices in a variety of "best of" categories. The results follow:

Best National Event
- Mardi Gras — New Orleans
- Pasadena Tournament of Roses Parade
- Macy's Thanksgiving Day Parade

Best Regional Event
- Boise River Festival
- Kentucky Derby Festival
- Seattle Seafair, and Sunfest of Palm Beach County (FL) (tie)

Best Sports Event
- Super Bowl
- Indianapolis 500
- The Olympics

Best Arts-related Event
- Cherry Creek Arts Festival
- Coconut Grove Arts Festival
- Houston International Festival

Most Prominent Sponsors
- Anheuser-Busch
- Coca-Cola
- Pepsi
- Miller Brewing Company, AT&T, Visa, Mastercard (tie)

Best Seminars/Conferences on Special Events and Event Marketing
- International Festivals & Events Association (IFEA) Annual Conference
- International Events Group (IEG) Sponsorship Conference
- IFEA Profits Seminar

While there are several smaller conferences that cover the topics, or parts of the topics, of events and sponsorship (e.g. IFEA State Associations, state tourism conferences, etc.), the two major sources of information for those we questioned were the International Festivals and Events Association (IFEA) and the International Events Group (IEG) annual conferences.

The IFEA is geared more specifically to festivals and events and was the first choice of those respondents who represent events. Its annual conference is held each September or October in different locations. The IFEA also hosts a number of other seminars on specific topics (e.g. parades, sponsorship, arts festivals, and smaller regional/state conferences) throughout the year. For more IFEA information contact:

Bruce Skinner
President
International Festivals & Events Association
P.O. Box 2950
1034 Caroline
Port Angeles, WA 98362-0336
Phone: (360) 457-3141
Fax: (360) 452-4695

The IEG Conference offers valuable information to everyone, but it is aimed most specifically at addressing the needs of the corporate sponsor. It was the first choice of those respondents who represented corporations or sponsoring entities.

For more information on the IEG contact:

Lesa Ukman
International Events Group, Inc.
640 North LaSalle, Suite 600
Chicago, IL 60610-3777
Phone: (312) 944-1727
Fax: (312) 944-1897

PREDICTIONS

How do members of the special events industry view the future? We asked for their input and they came back with the following reflections. We have also included some thoughts from an interview with industry members by the IEG Sponsorship Report.

- Partnership between events and sponsors, other events, causes, cities, retailers, and the media will become necessities to our continued and mutual success.
- Technology and the world-wide web will bring sweeping new opportunities for both events and sponsors to reach/service audiences.
- Multiculturalism and diversity will be an issue with event programming, management, boards and more.
- Events will feel the squeeze as host cities struggle to recover costs and donate less services.
- Highly visible events will become the center of more and more political and legal issues.
- Events will have to work harder to hold the attention of a more sophisticated audience.
- A greater sense of professionalism will sweep through the industry, and days of "spare time" event management will be gone.
- Events will struggle to provide "safe havens" for event-goers, especially in larger urban markets.
- "Survival of the fittest" rule will take place, with fewer quality events enjoying stronger corporate support.
- Events will be expected to provide recycling/ environmental programs on-site.
- Sales will drive most sponsorship decisions and serve as the number one evaluation method.

- Events will necessarily package sponsorships to include more advertising, opportunities for employee involvement, and other direct, sponsor-specific benefits.
- The special events industry will continue to experience greater growth overall as businesses, which have become so large, try to recapture the ability to reach out and touch the consumer.
- Special events will become more tightly targeted to specific audiences, and there will be less clutter to avoid confusing sponsor messages.
- Events must become more cost effective and offer greater benefits for sponsors.
- The future will see more advertising agencies becoming involved in event marketing as clients demand it.
- Producers will create events in the sponsor's image to help guarantee support.
- Family-oriented events will become more important.
- Sponsor dollars will grow slower than the demand for those dollars, creating a need within events for more creativity, better packaging, higher attendance, and more ways to meet sponsor objectives.
- The industry will become more internally specialized with fewer suppliers trying to do everything.
- Older events will need to find new ways to stay fresh as the competition increases.
- Sponsor interest will create a need for stronger local events.
- Corporate sponsors will necessarily add personnel to their corporate event departments.
- We will see dazzling innovation in the creation of mammoth events, some global in scope, on a scale heretofore unknown.
- Global properties will have an increasingly higher profile as major international companies look for events to help them cross borders and oceans.
- Cross-promotions among sponsors will increase.

- Corporate takeovers will have a major impact on events currently sponsored by takeover targets.
- Event sponsorships will replace philanthropy somewhat as sponsorship dollars work harder to produce benefits to the corporation, the organization, and the community at large.
- Special events will be used more and more by cities and states to support economic development.
- Venue sponsorship will increase.
- Adaptations of "ambush marketing" will increase. Those evaluating future sponsorships will need to consider potential ambushers — namely, the sponsor's competitors—in their marketing plans.
- Events will need to provide greater hospitality opportunities for sponsors.
- Television coverage (especially cable) of more varied events, including regional and local events, will increase.
- Television and cable networks will copy Ted Turner's concept of owning and packaging the Goodwill Games. This approach offers a sponsorship promotion and media buy all in one.
- Event Marketing and Management will be offered in formalized degree programs at the university level.
- There will be fewer umbrella sponsorships and more product-specific sponsorships that allow for on- and off-site tie-ins.
- Measurement and evaluation standards will improve, helping to legitimize special events sponsorship.
- A professional association with an established code of ethics will bind the industry together.

Whatever the future holds, it is an exciting time to be a part of this very exciting industry! We wish everyone the very best in their endeavors and hope that we have helped to make all of your events even more special.

ABOUT THE AUTHORS

STEVEN WOOD SCHMADER, CFE, is the President of the Boise River Festival, which started from scratch in 1991. Today, with the support of more than 750 sponsors and 3,700 volunteers, the Festival features more than 400 events and reaches an aggregate attendance of over one million. The Boise River Festival has been recognized as one of the "Top 100 Events in North America"; "Top 40 Events in the Country"; "Top 10 Summer Festivals in the United States"; and "Top 3 New Events, Worldwide, Created in the Last Ten Years."

Schmader also holds the position of Executive Director of NCAA college football's newest bowl game, the "Sports Humanitarian Bowl", played in Boise, and for which the Boise River Festival serves as the managing organization.

Previously Schmader spent twelve years in the special events industry working for Up With People as their Director of Special Events.

His many credits include the direction of Up With People's 25th Anniversary "Silver Celebration"; the "Welcome Home Celebration" for released U.S. hostage Jess "Jon" Turner; the annual induction ceremonies for the World Sports Humanitarian Hall of Fame; the opening of the 60th Annual Macy's Thanksgiving Day parade; the Washington D.C. Fourth of July "Celebration on the Mall"; and the event team for Super Bowl XX in New Orleans.

Schmader is the Chairman-Elect of the International Festivals & Events Association (IFEA) and a Past President of the Rocky Mountain Festivals & Events Association, which he helped found. The co-author of this book, the complete IFEA library of resources and *Building Marketing Alliances* (published by the International Council of Air Shows), Schmader is a frequent and highly rated speaker on industry-related topics.

ROBERT JACKSON has actually had concurrent careers in special events and publicity. He began both when on the staff of the Walt Disney organization, starting at WED Enterprises, Inc., then a company personally owned by Walt Disney. WED and its subsequent repositioning as a Walt Disney company, planned, designed, and supervised construction of all Disney theme parks and their later-added attractions.

Following Disney's death, Jackson relocated to Disneyland where, as Publicity Manager, he was involved in the planning and implementation of the California theme park's many special events.

He then joined the federal government as Director of Media Services for the (now titled) United States Travel and Tourism Administration in the Department of Commerce. His role called for considerable involvement with special events and their producers throughout the nation, events being a primary instrument for attracting foreign tourists and encouraging within-nation travel by U.S. residents.

Still with the government, Jackson moved into the position of Director of Public Relations and Advertising for the John F. Kennedy Center for the Performing Arts in Washington, D.C. Again, his duties included pivotal participation in the Center's extensive special events programming.

Later, at General Mills, Inc., he was Manager of Product Publicity and Event Marketing for the company's more than 200 brand units. Jackson planned a number of events for General Mills and created its system for processing an average of more than 4,000 sponsorship proposal annually.

In recent years, Jackson has served national companies and agencies as an independent special events and publicity consultant. He suspended agency operations to accept the two-year post of Special Events Manager for the 1991 International Special Olympics Games played in Minneapolis/St. Paul, Minnesota. Since 1992, he has been affiliated with INNOVA Marketing, Minneapolis, Minnesota.